To Our Wonderful Colorists,

This coloring book is dedicated to each and every one of you, our cherished colorists. Your creativity and passion for art have brought these zoo animal mandalas to life in the most vibrant and enchanting ways.

As you immerse yourself in this captivating journey of colors and patterns, know that your presence fills our hearts with gratitude. Your dedication to exploring the beauty of this world through your artistic expressions inspires us endlessly.

In every stroke of your colored pencils, in every gentle shading of your markers, you weave magic onto these pages, transforming them into masterpieces.

Your commitment to mindfulness and relaxation through coloring is truly admirable. With each completed artwork, you create a sanctuary of peace within yourself and radiate positivity into the world.

Thank you for embarking on this adventure with us. Your support and love have made this zoo mandala coloring book a reality. May your artistic endeavors continue to flourish, and may your heart always find joy in the art you create.
With heartfelt appreciation,
Margie Byrne

This book belongs to

_____

Wolf

Polar Bear

Red Panda

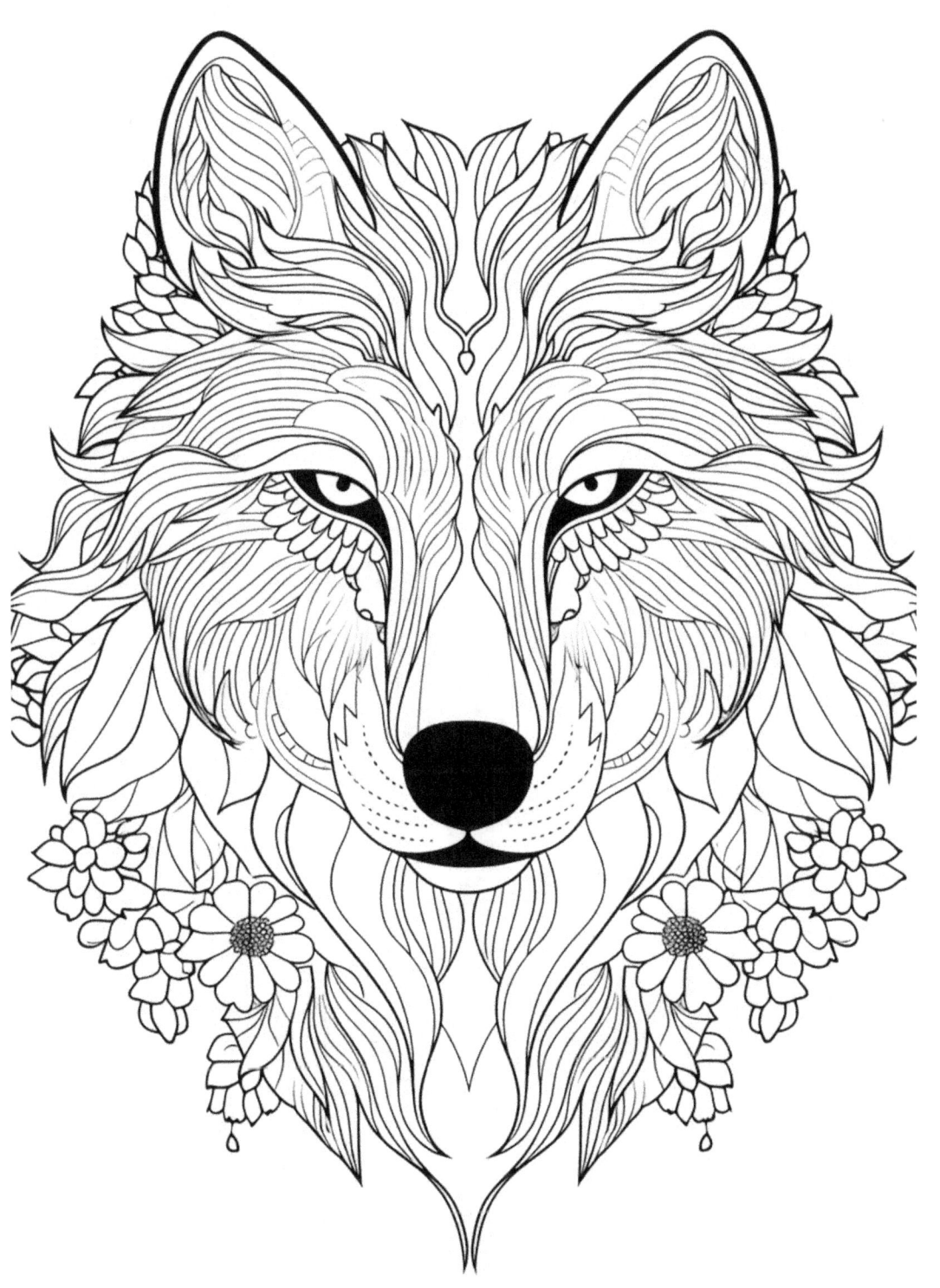

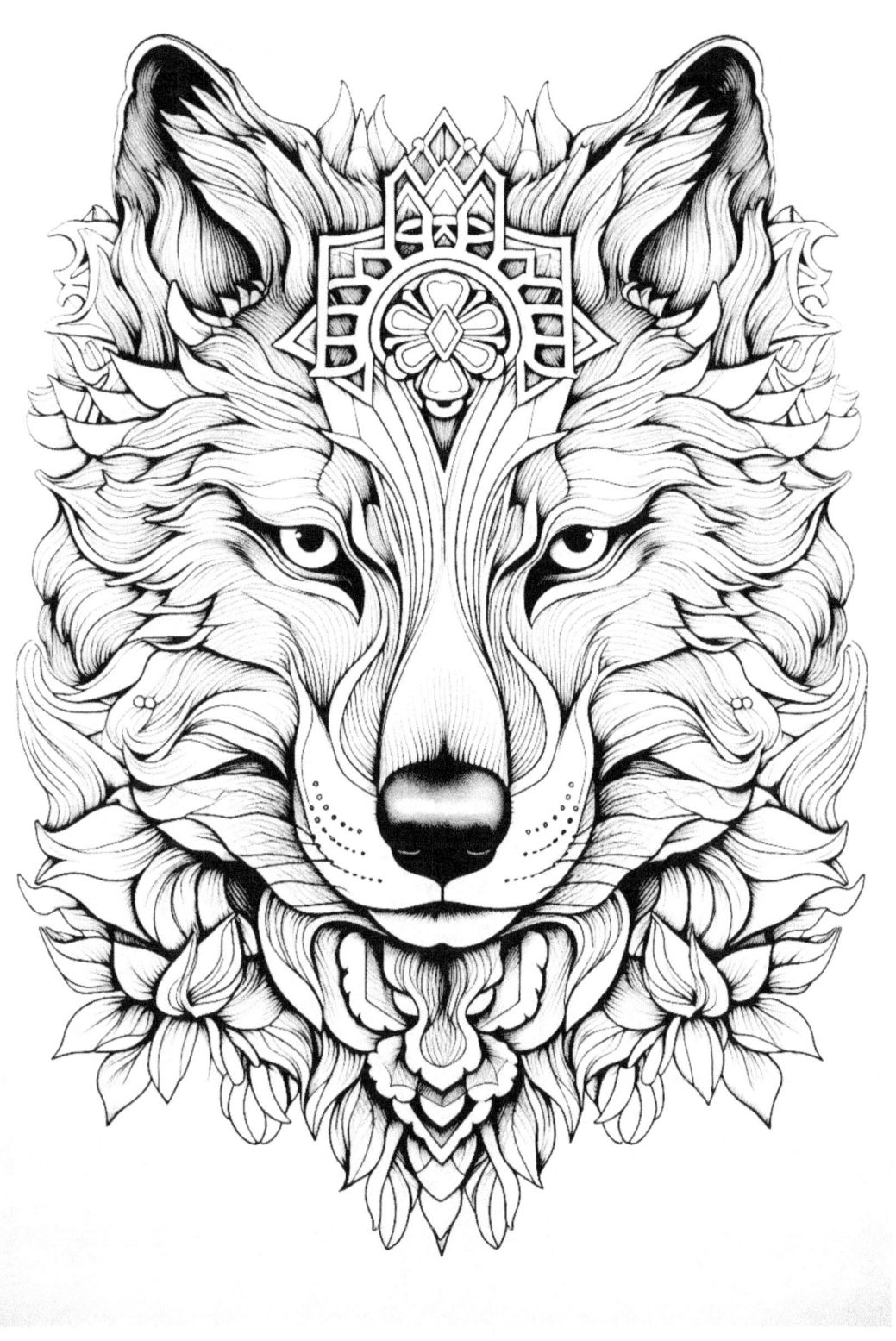

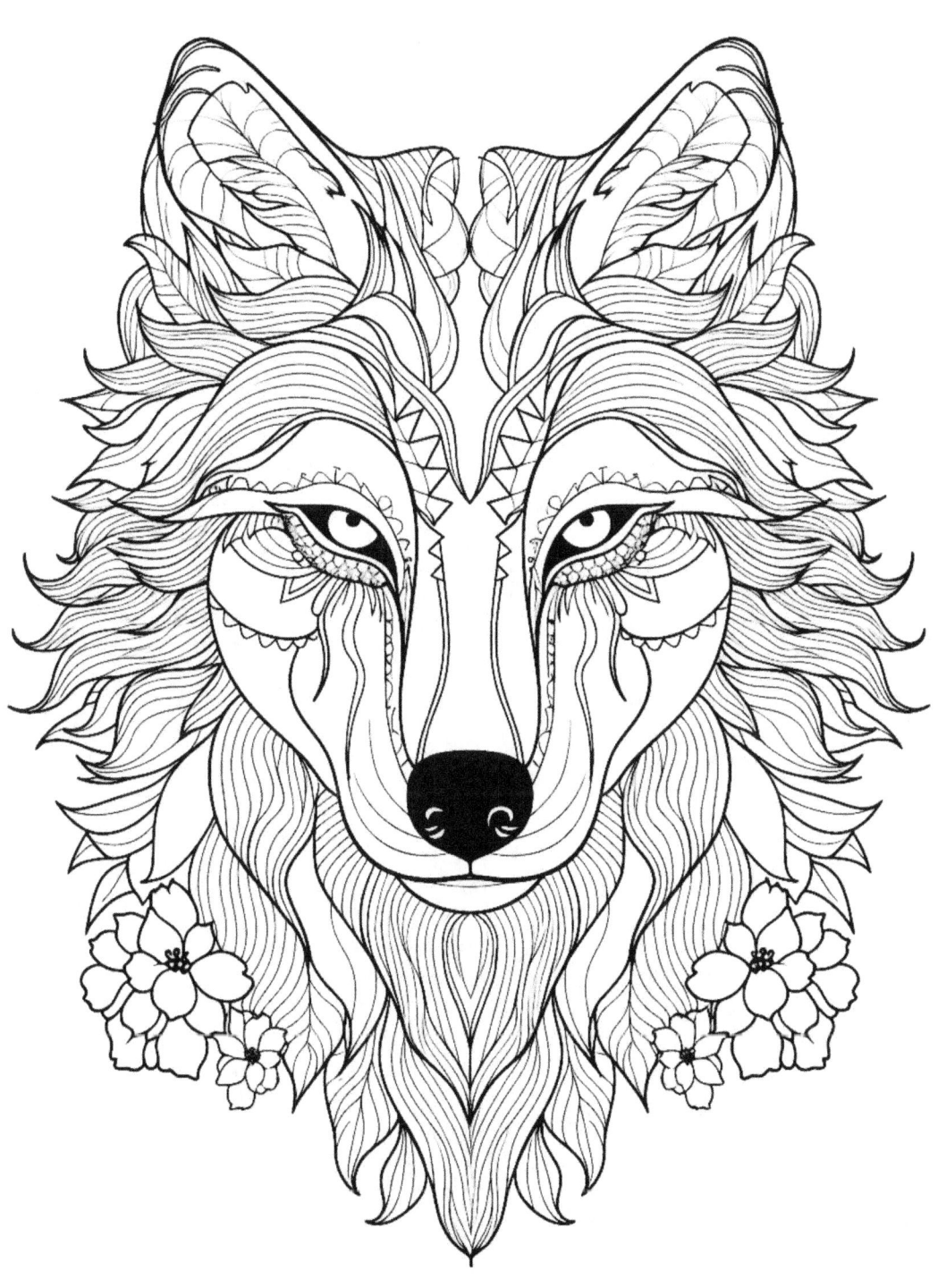

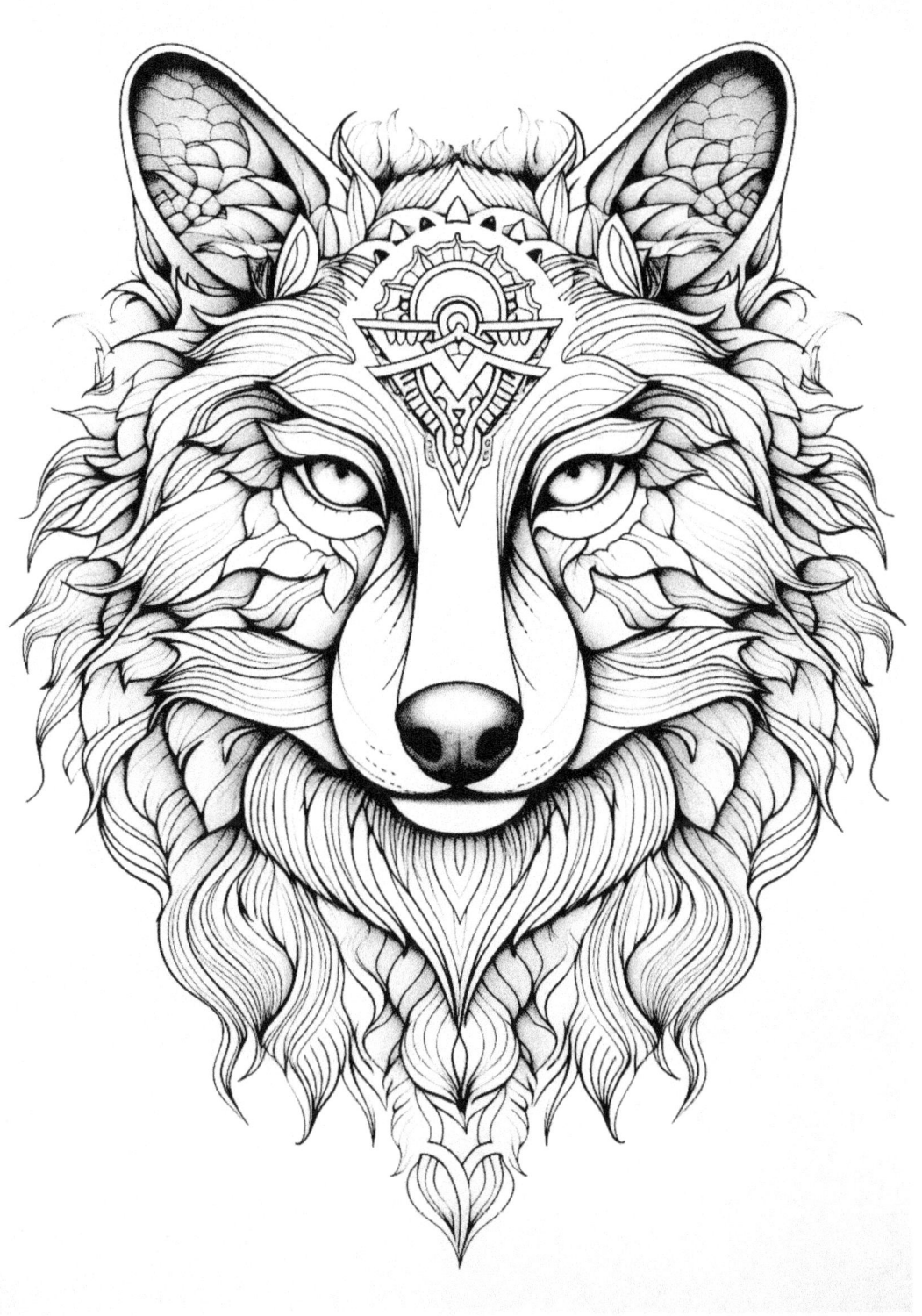

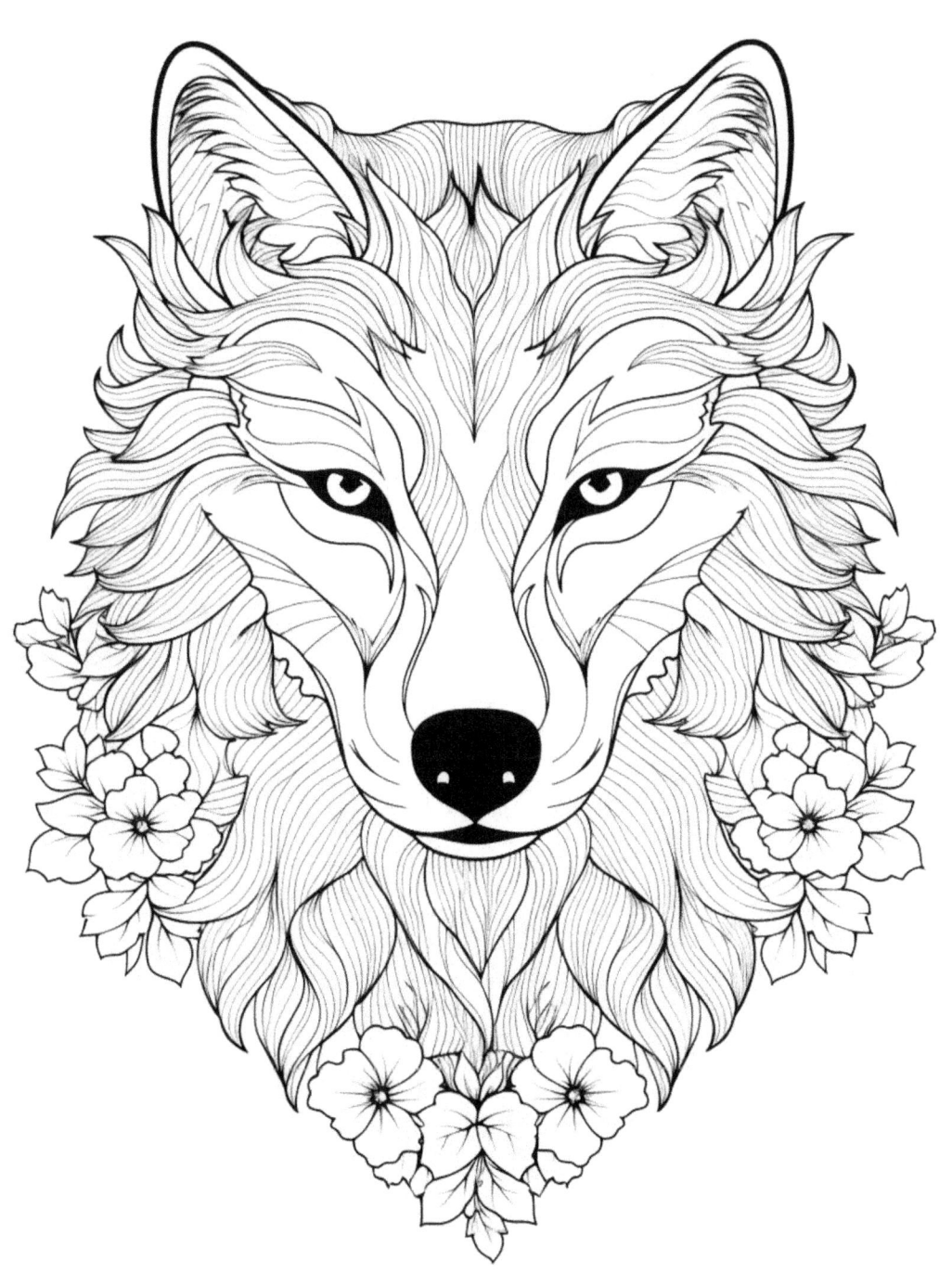

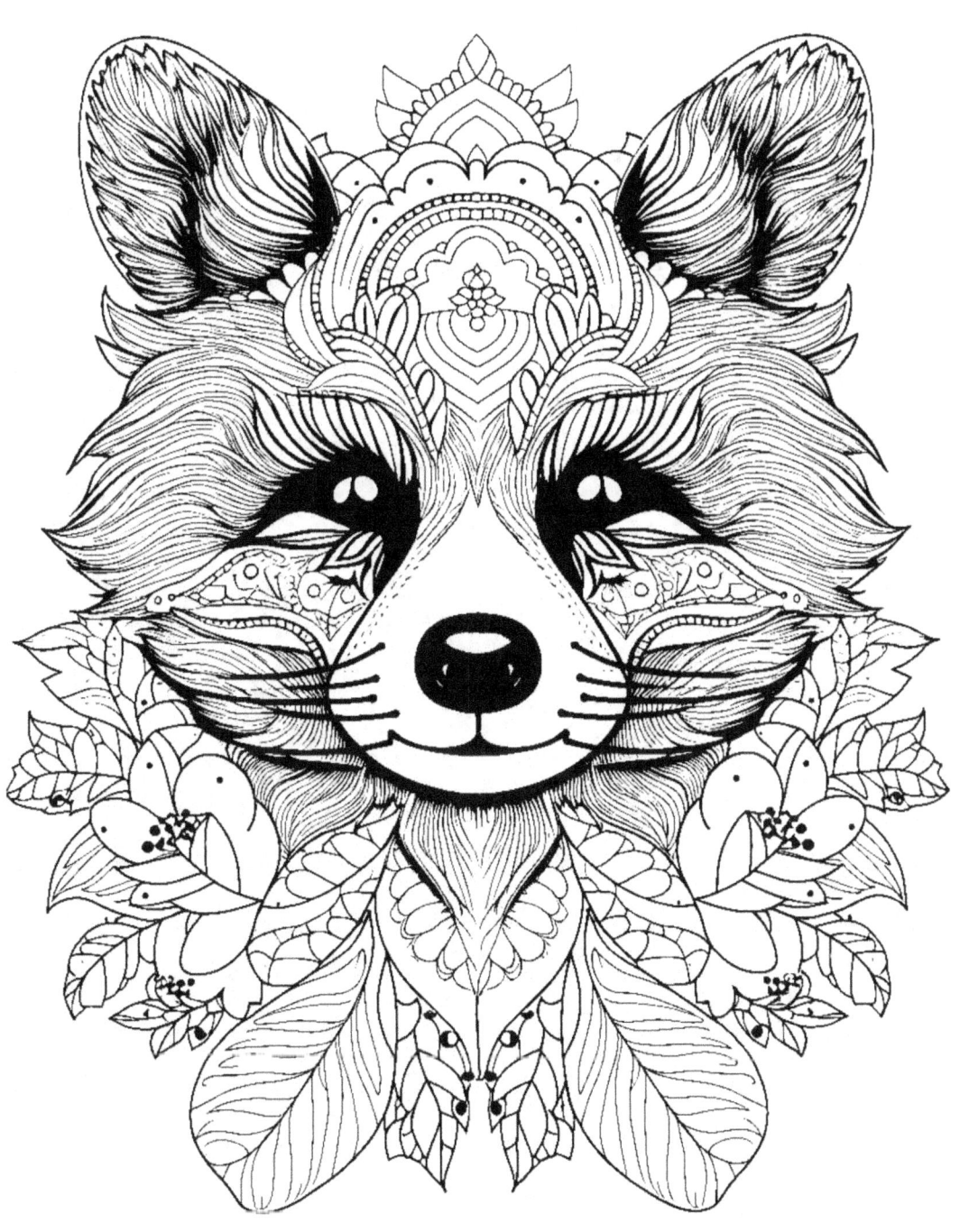

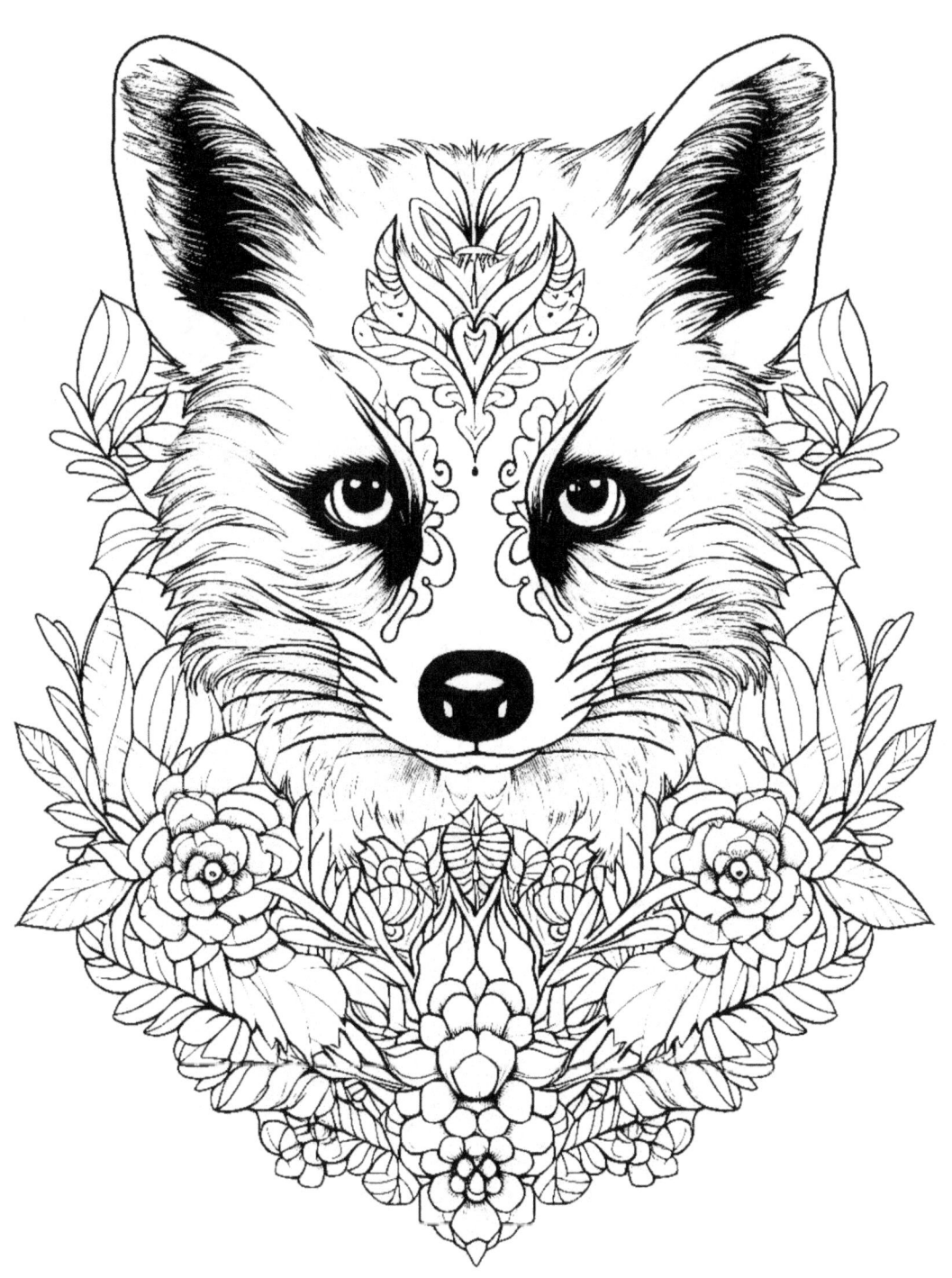

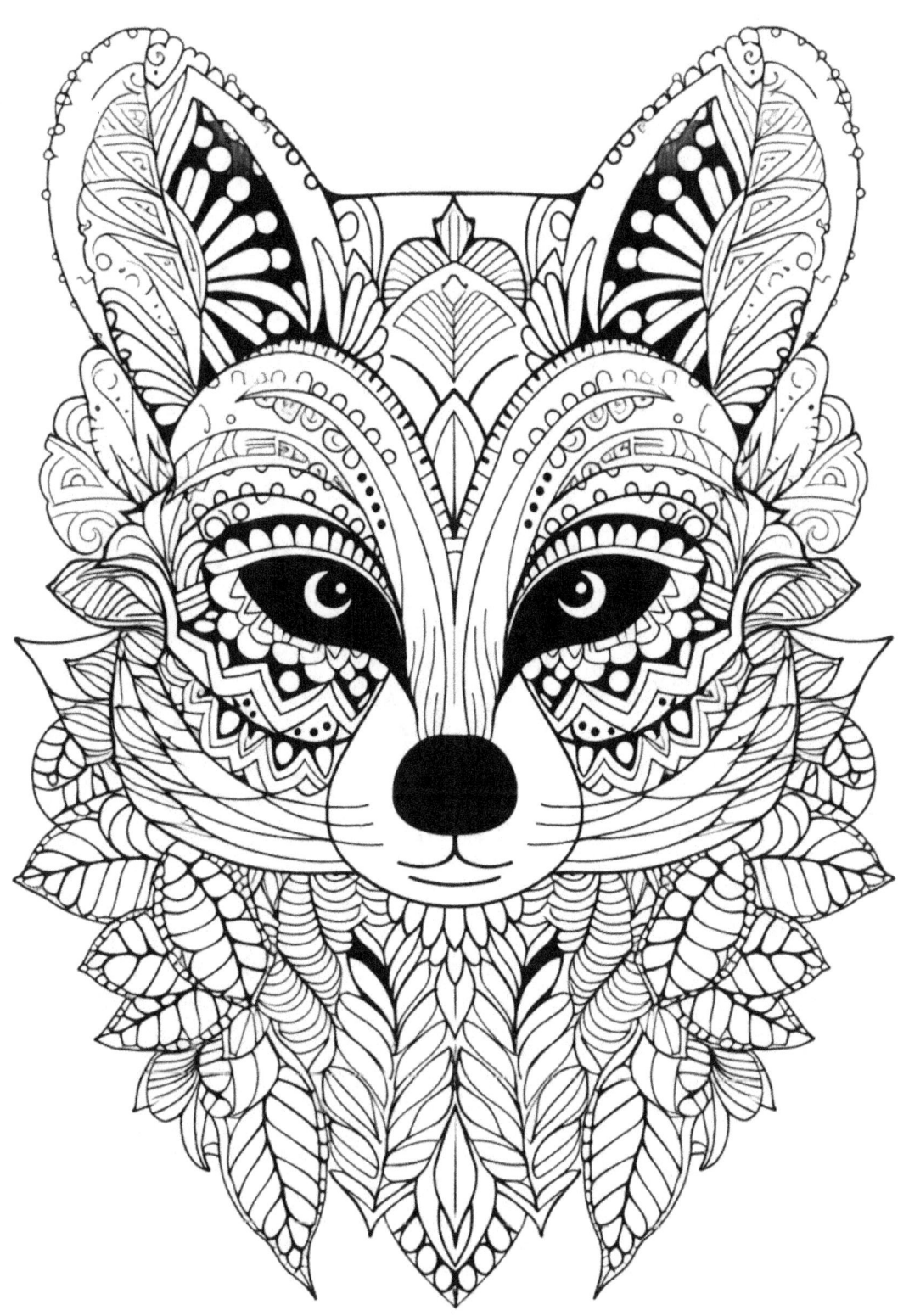

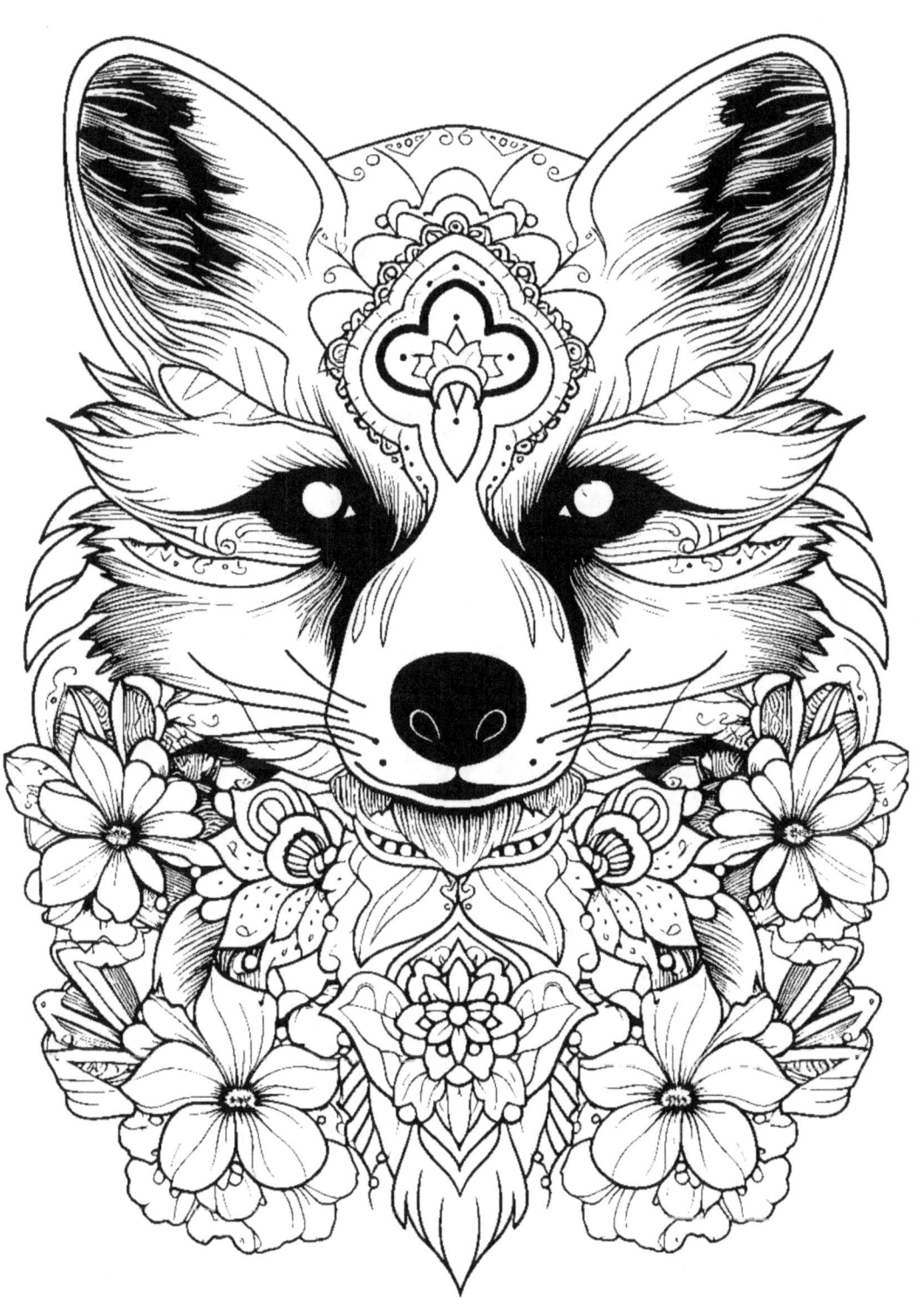

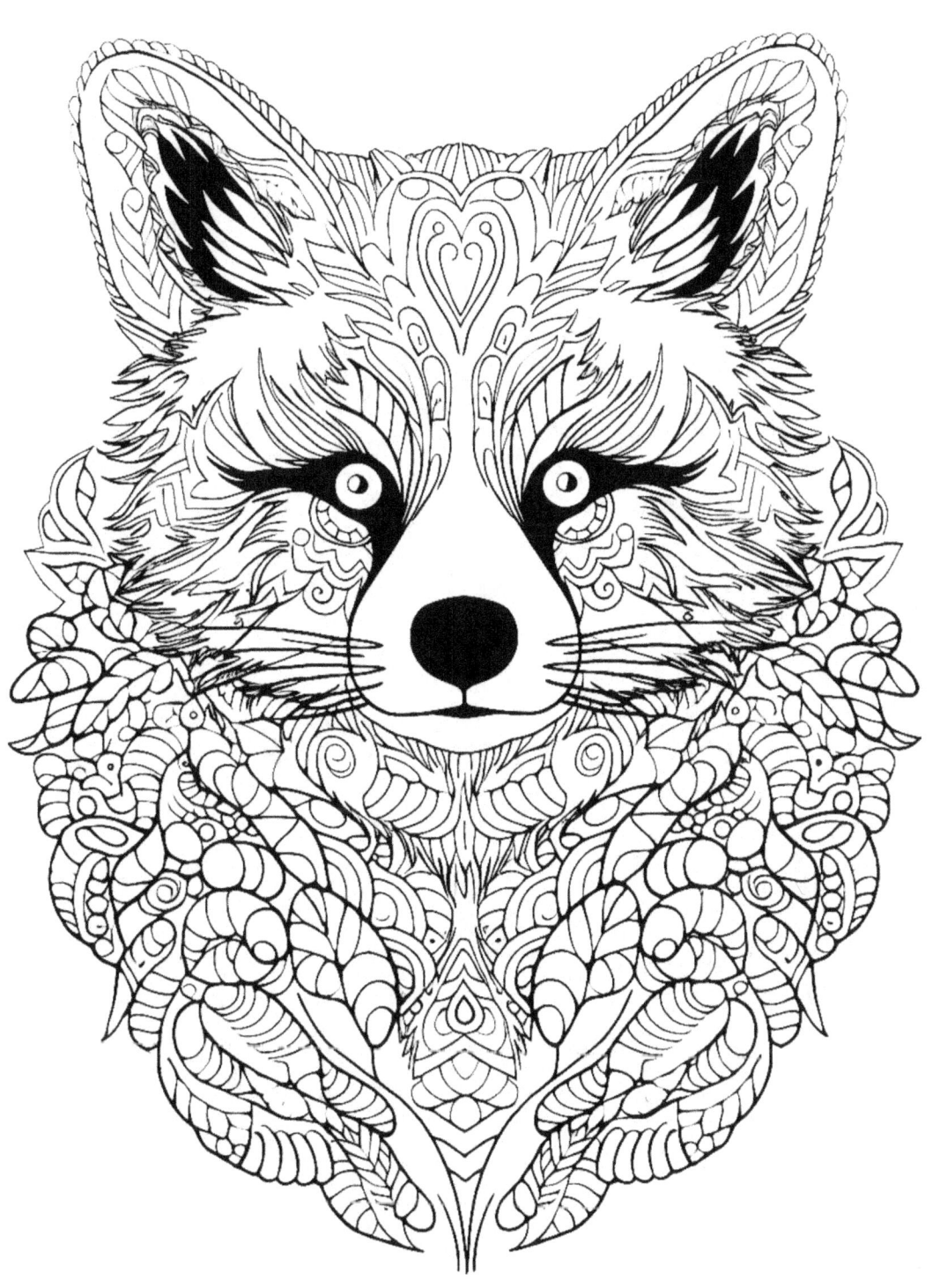

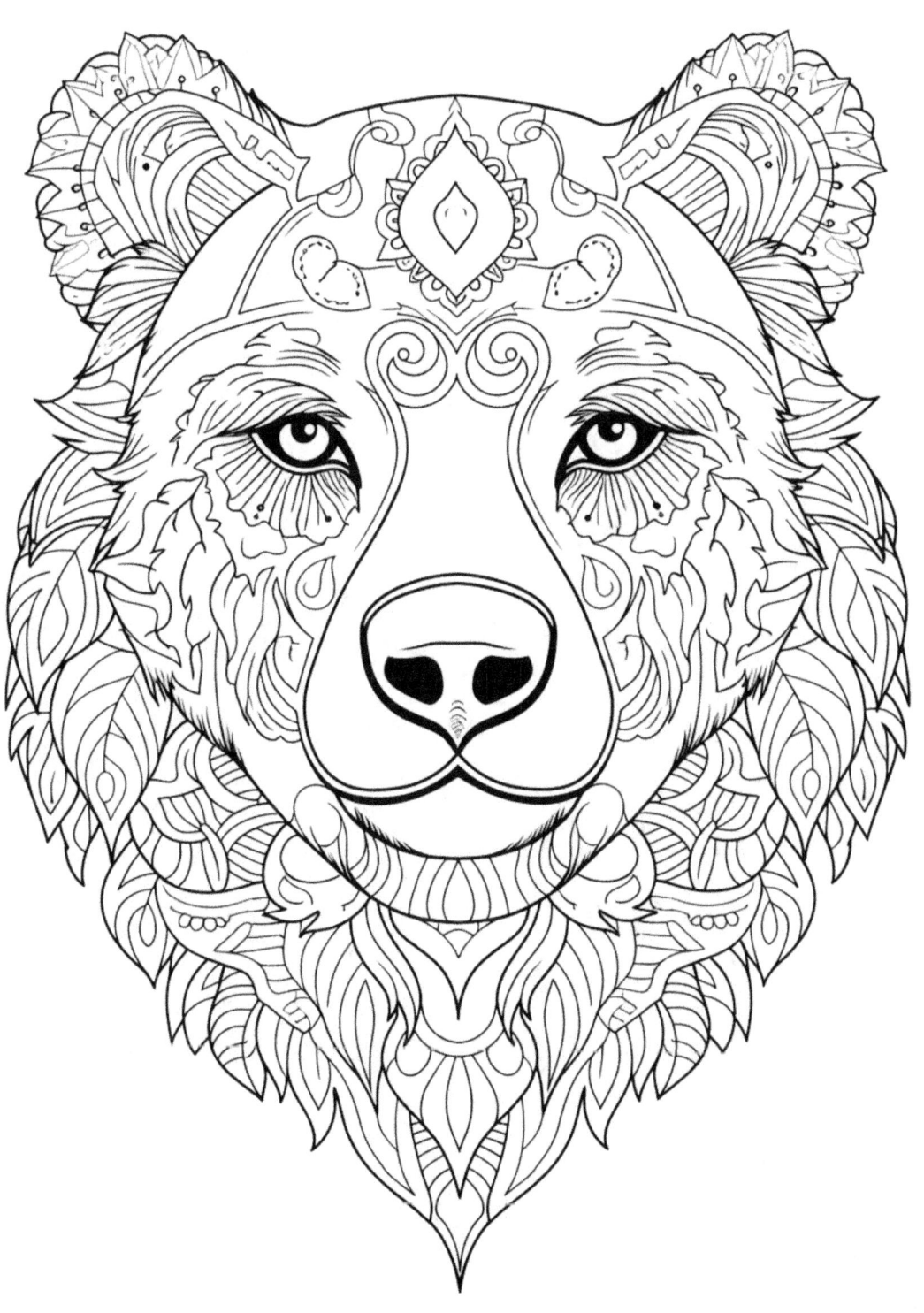

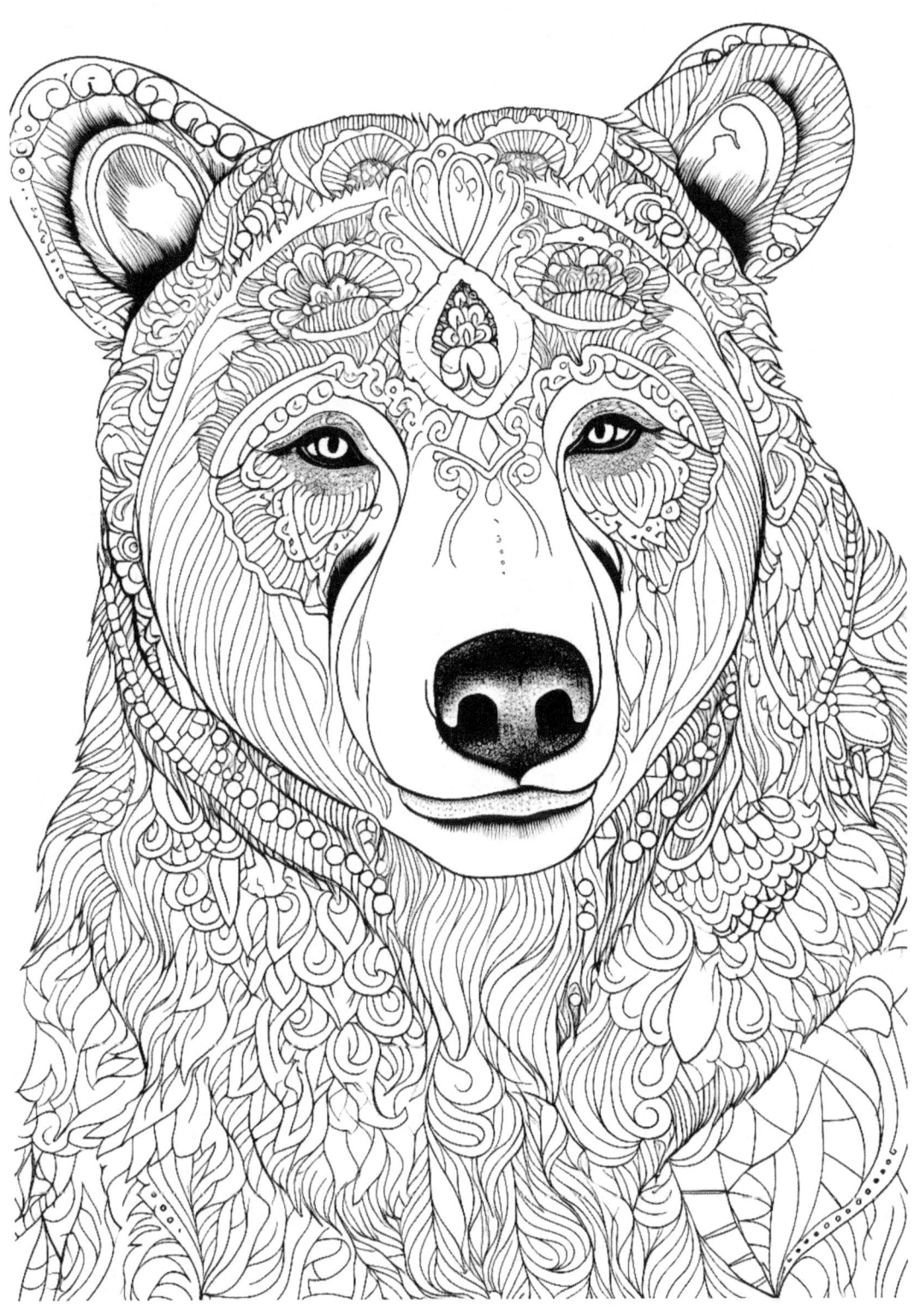

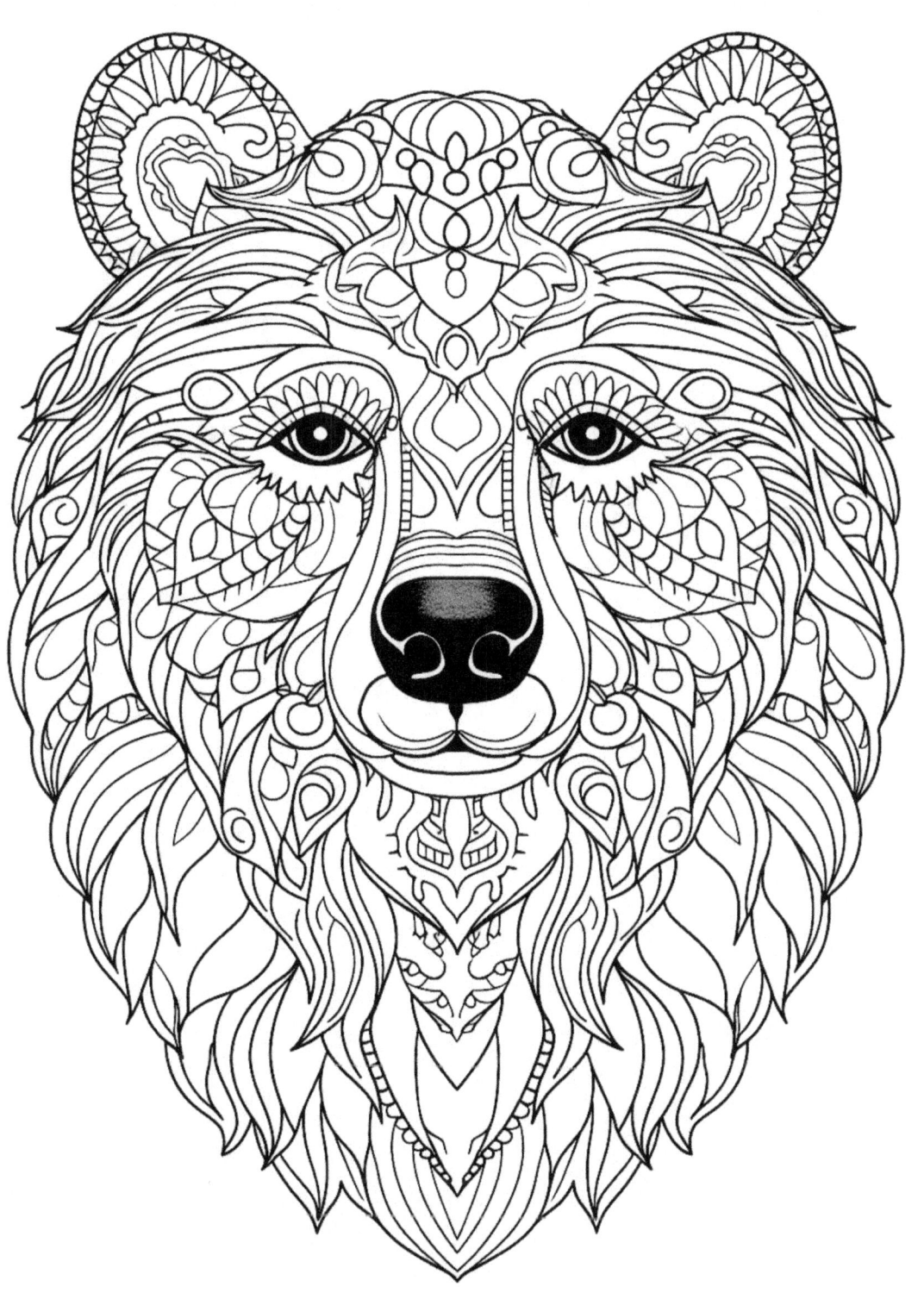

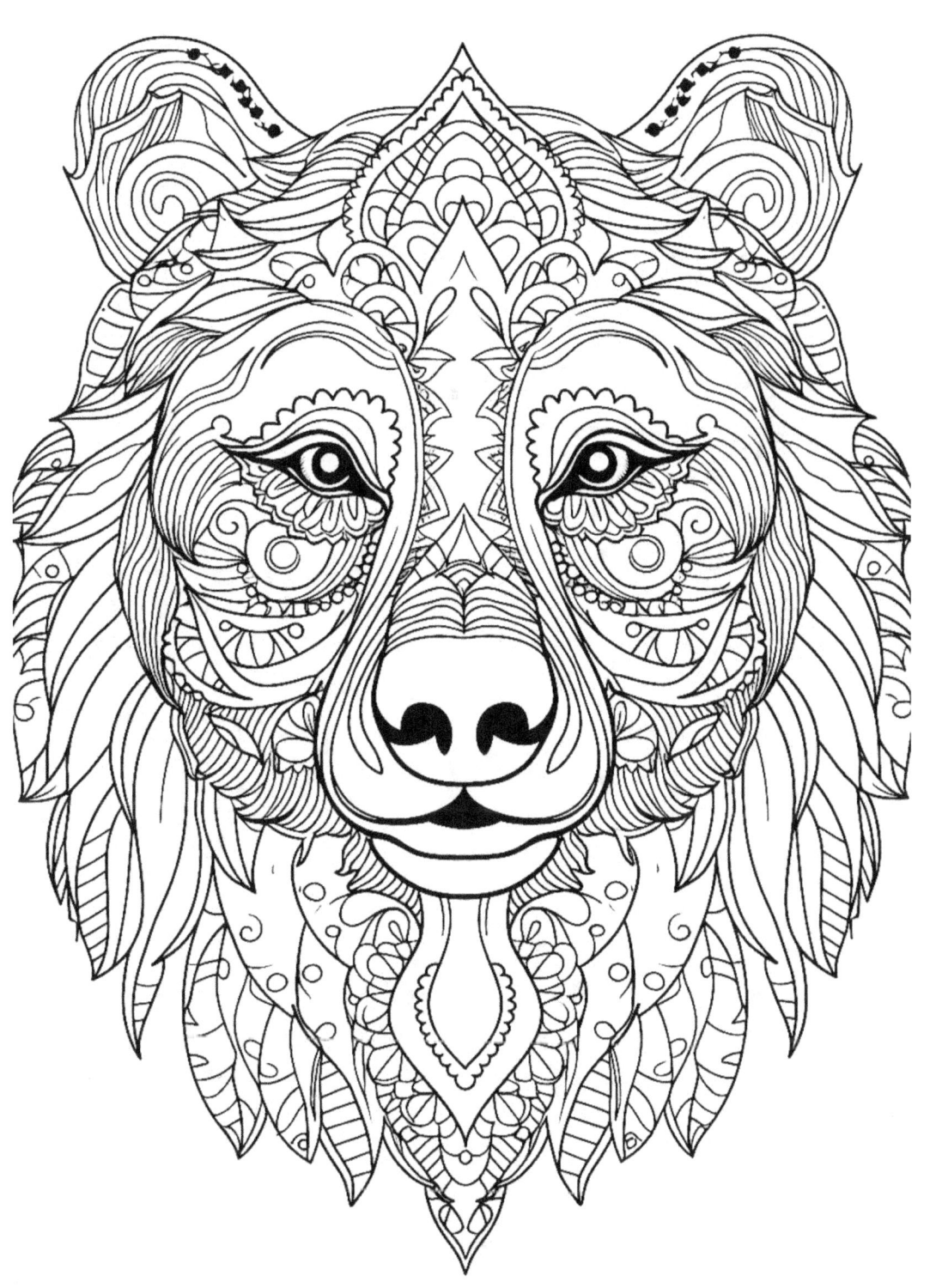

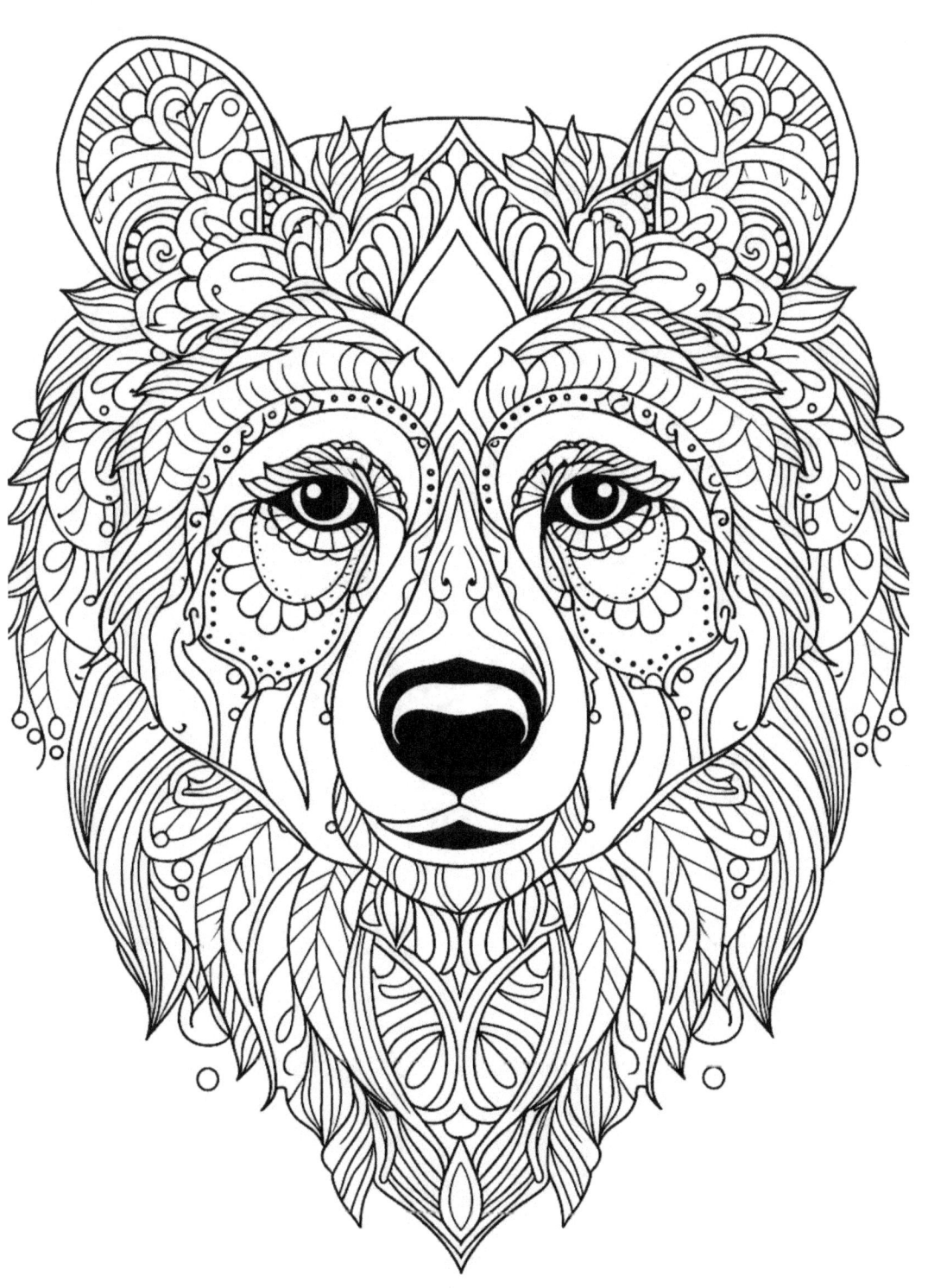

Cheetah
Lion
Tiger

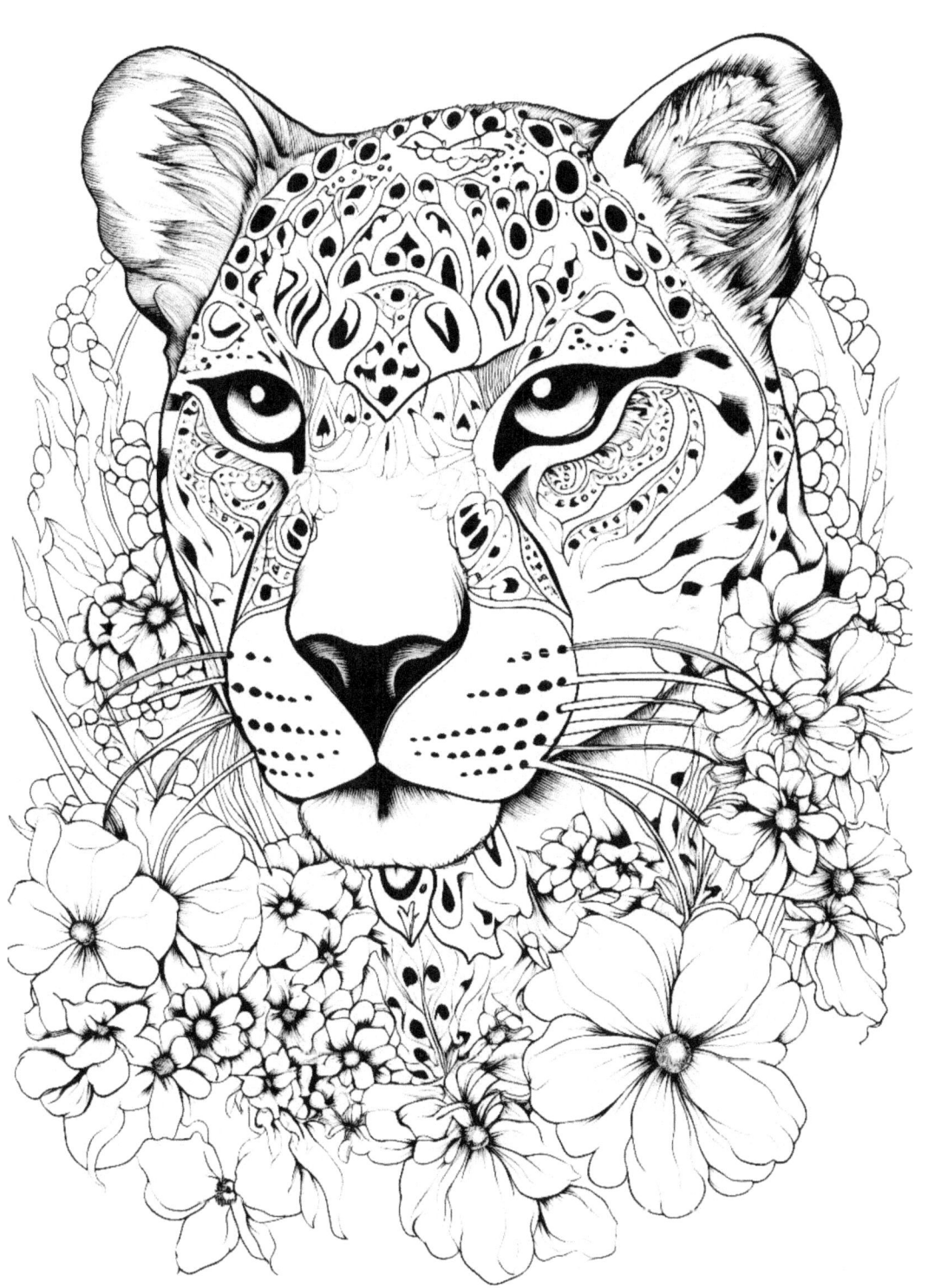

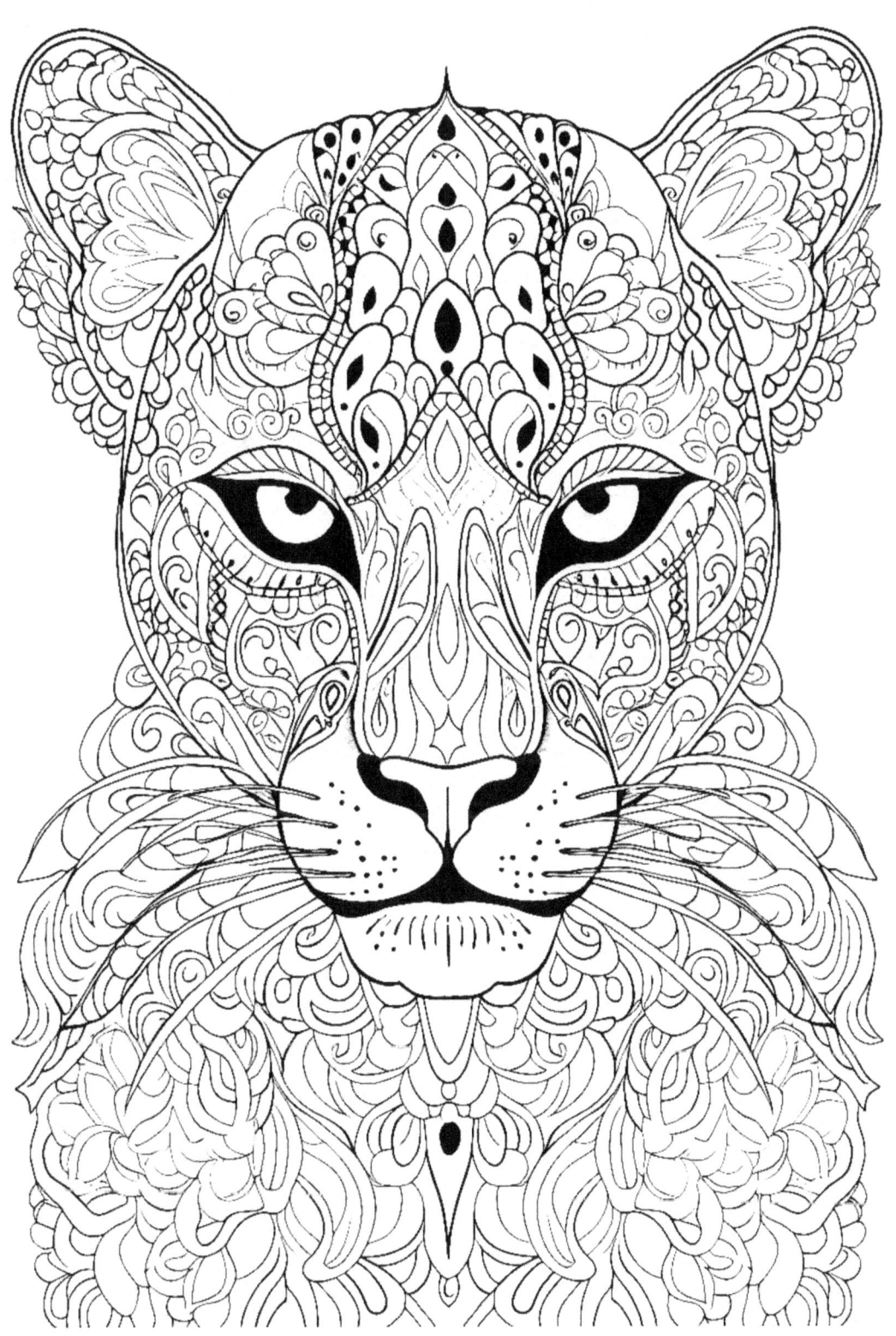

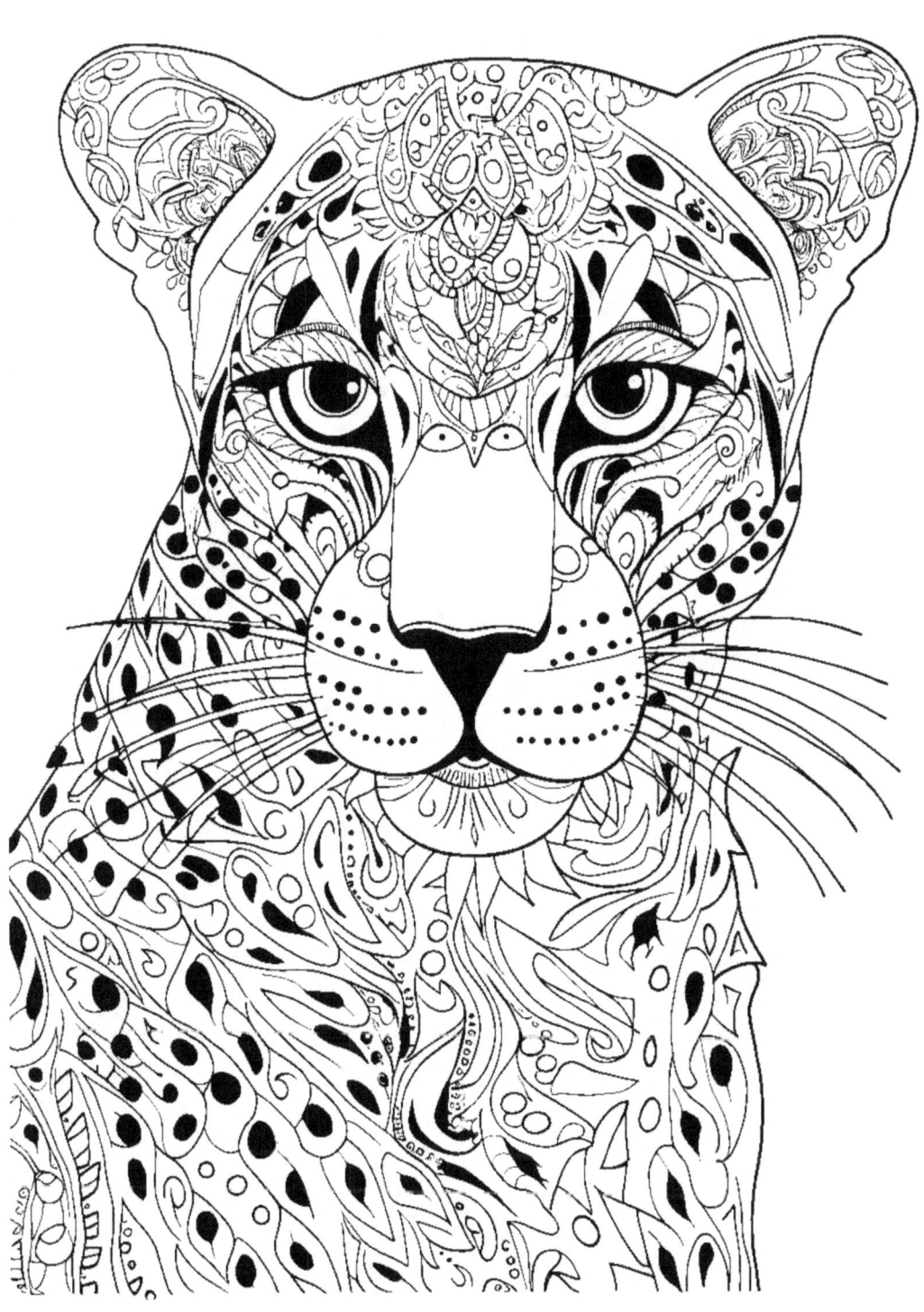

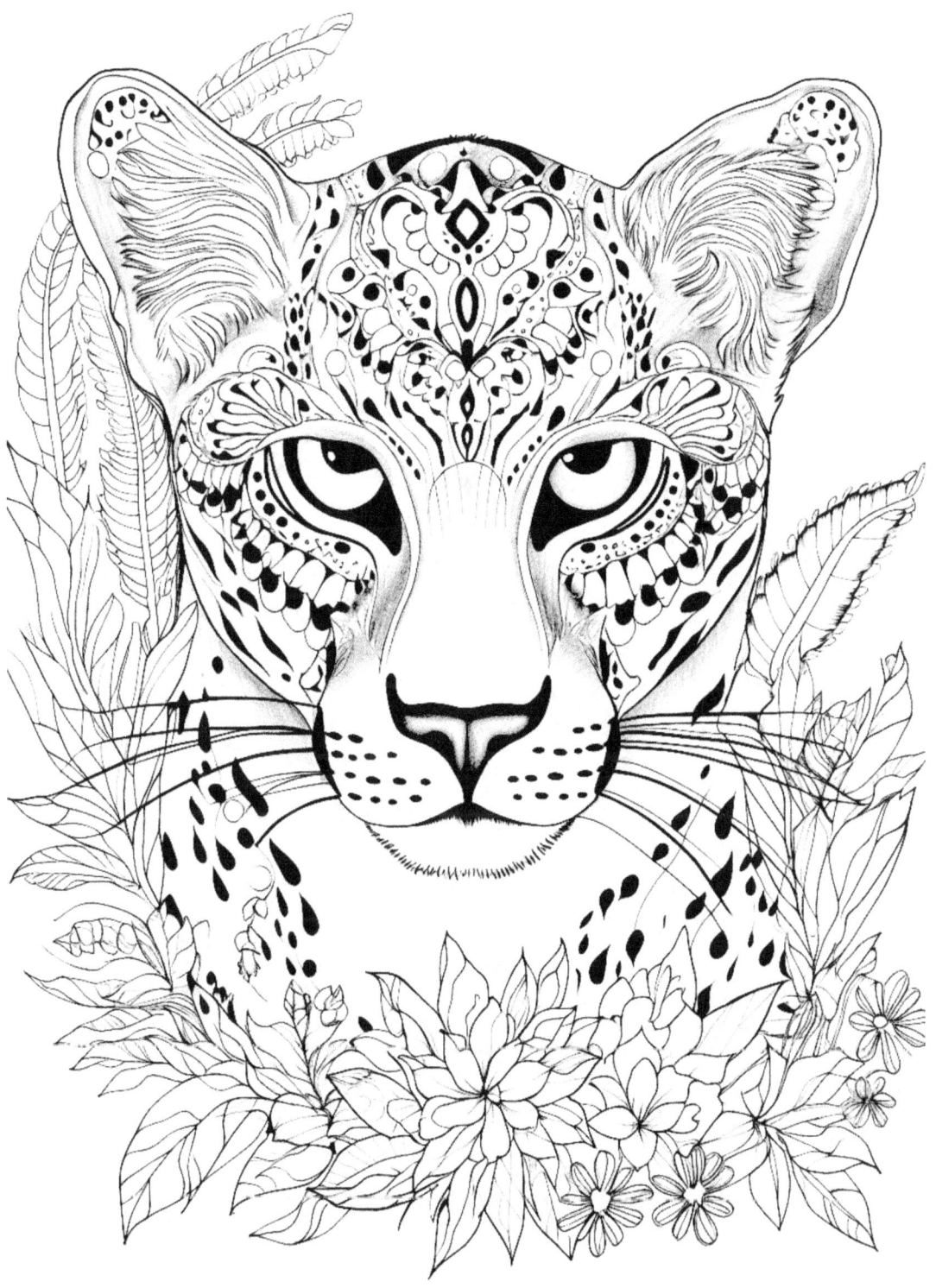

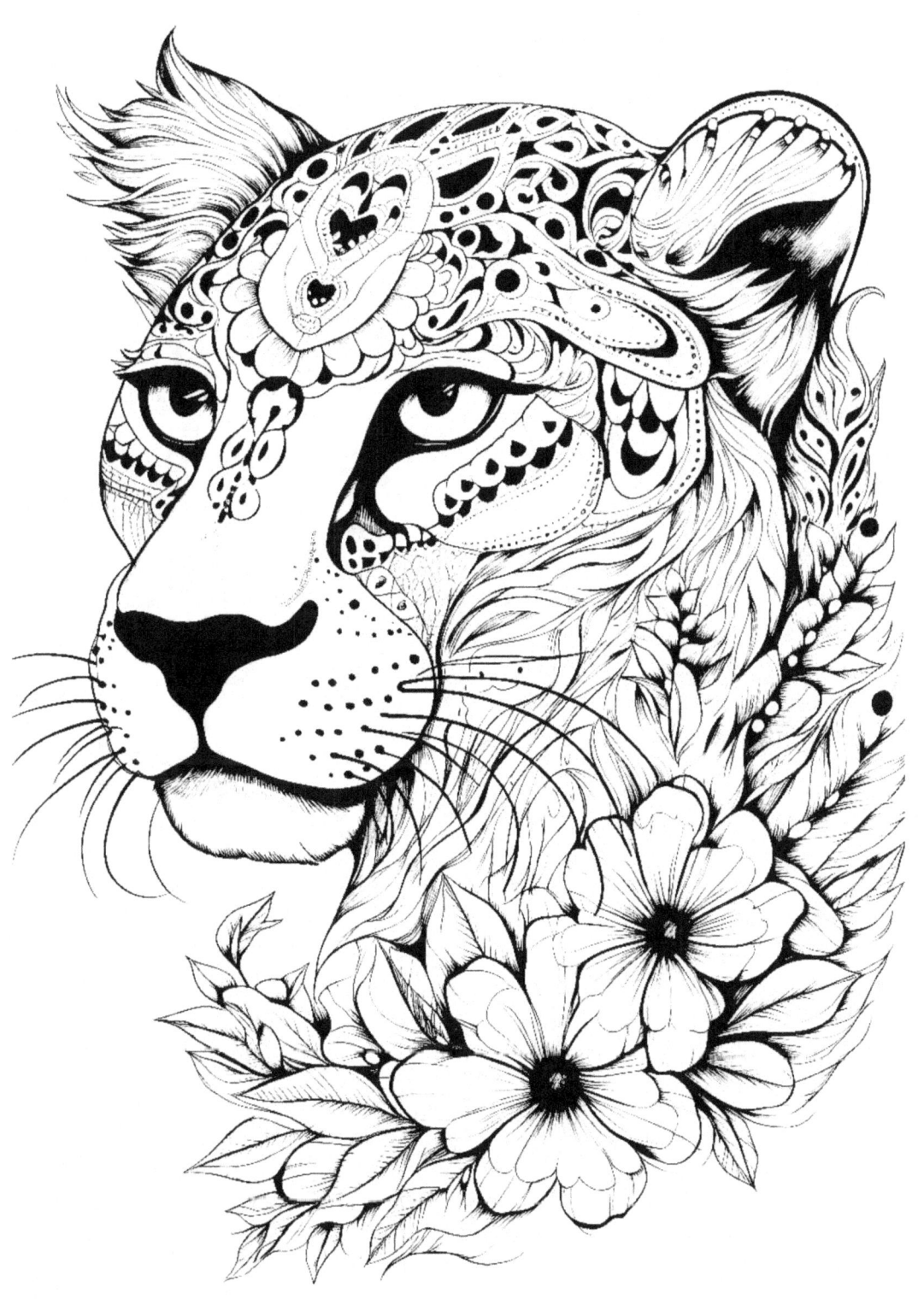

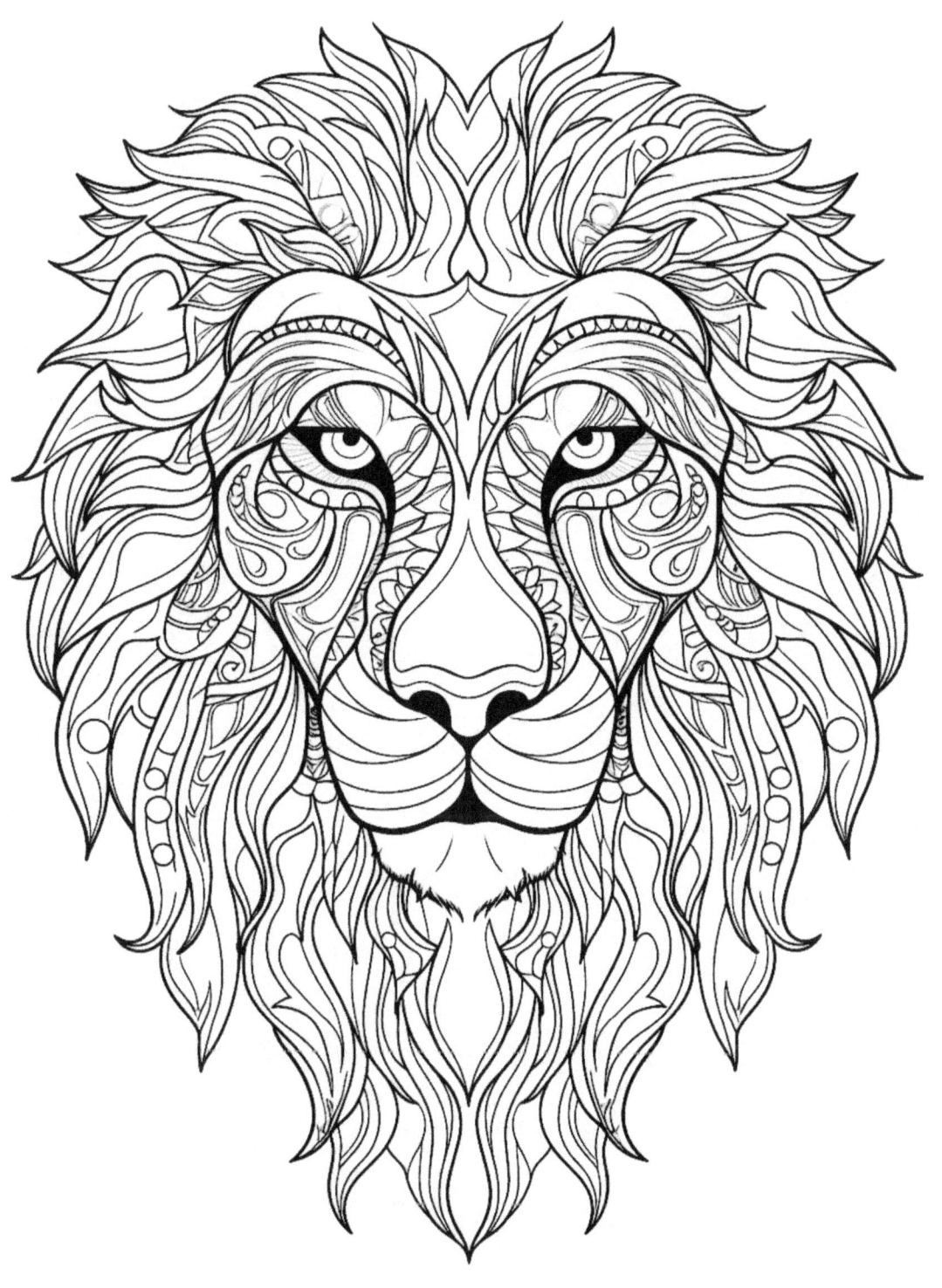

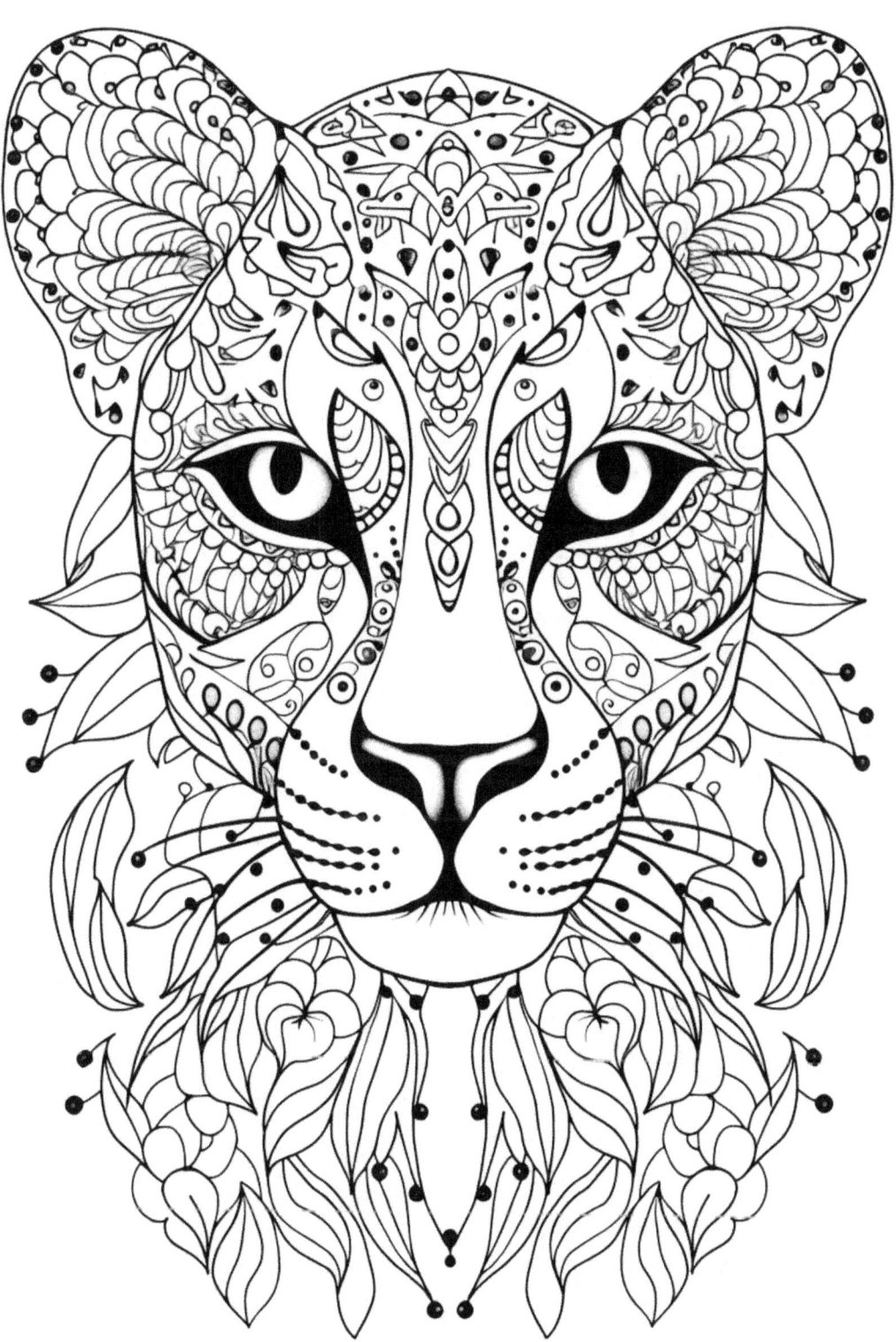

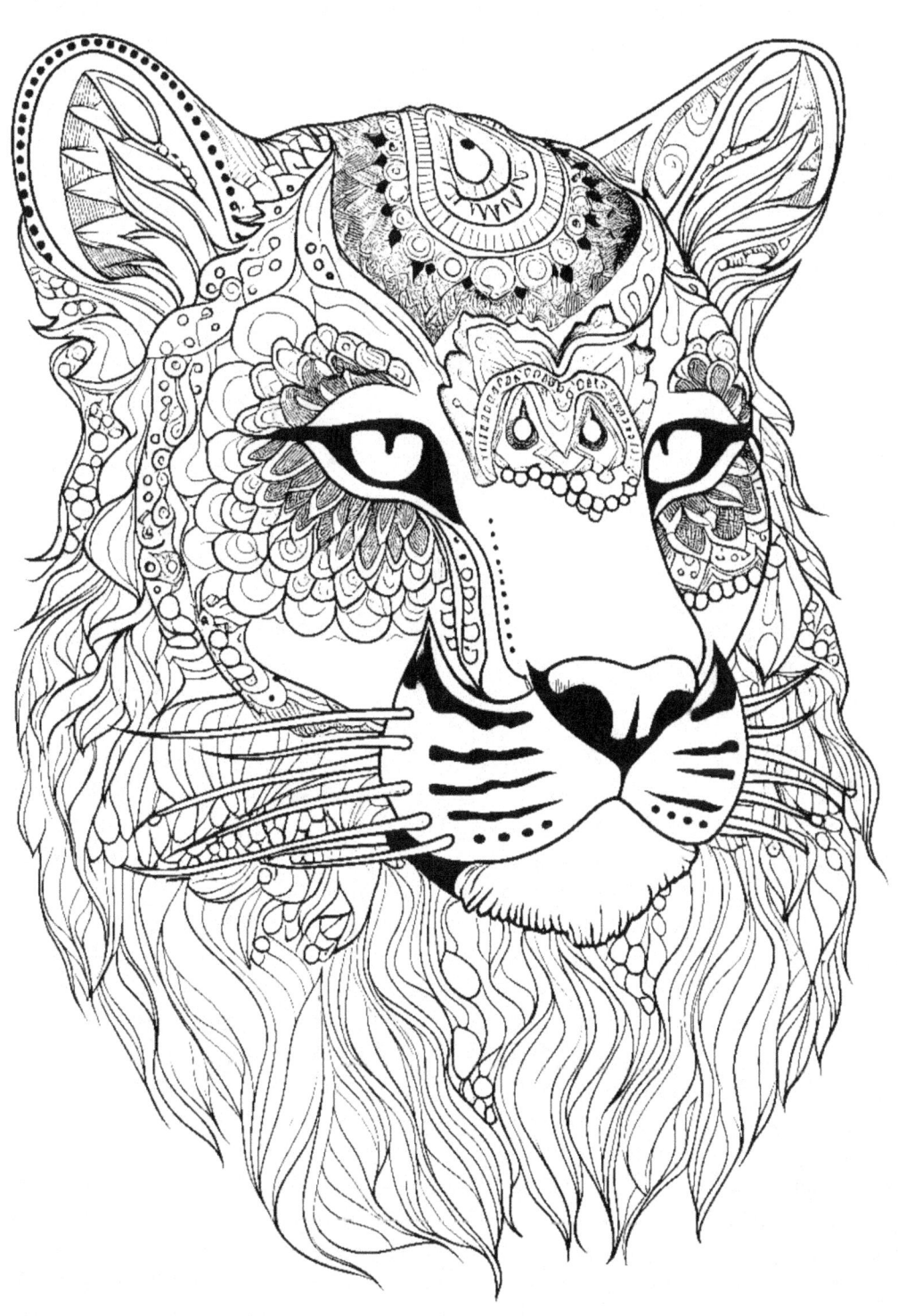

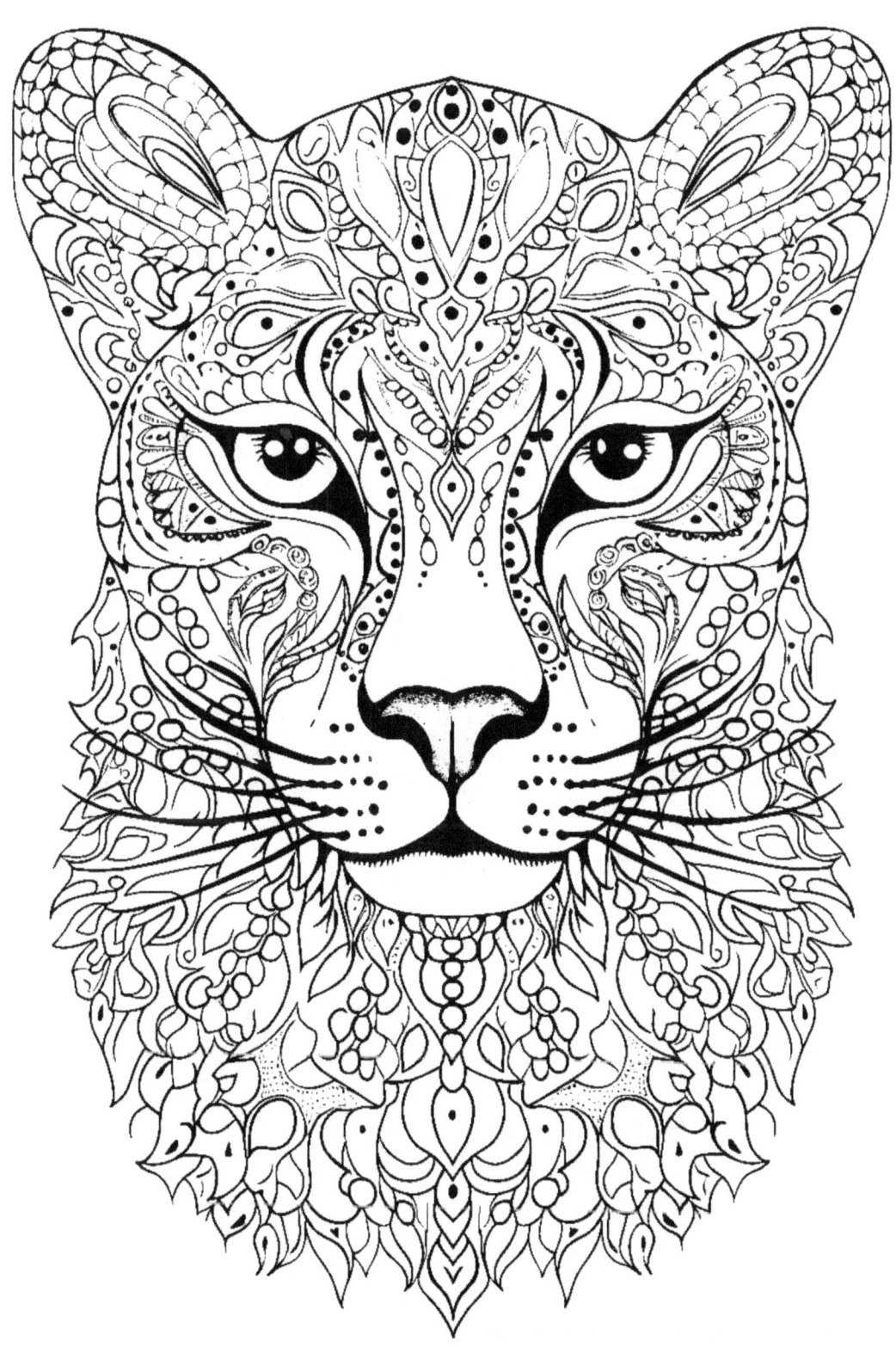

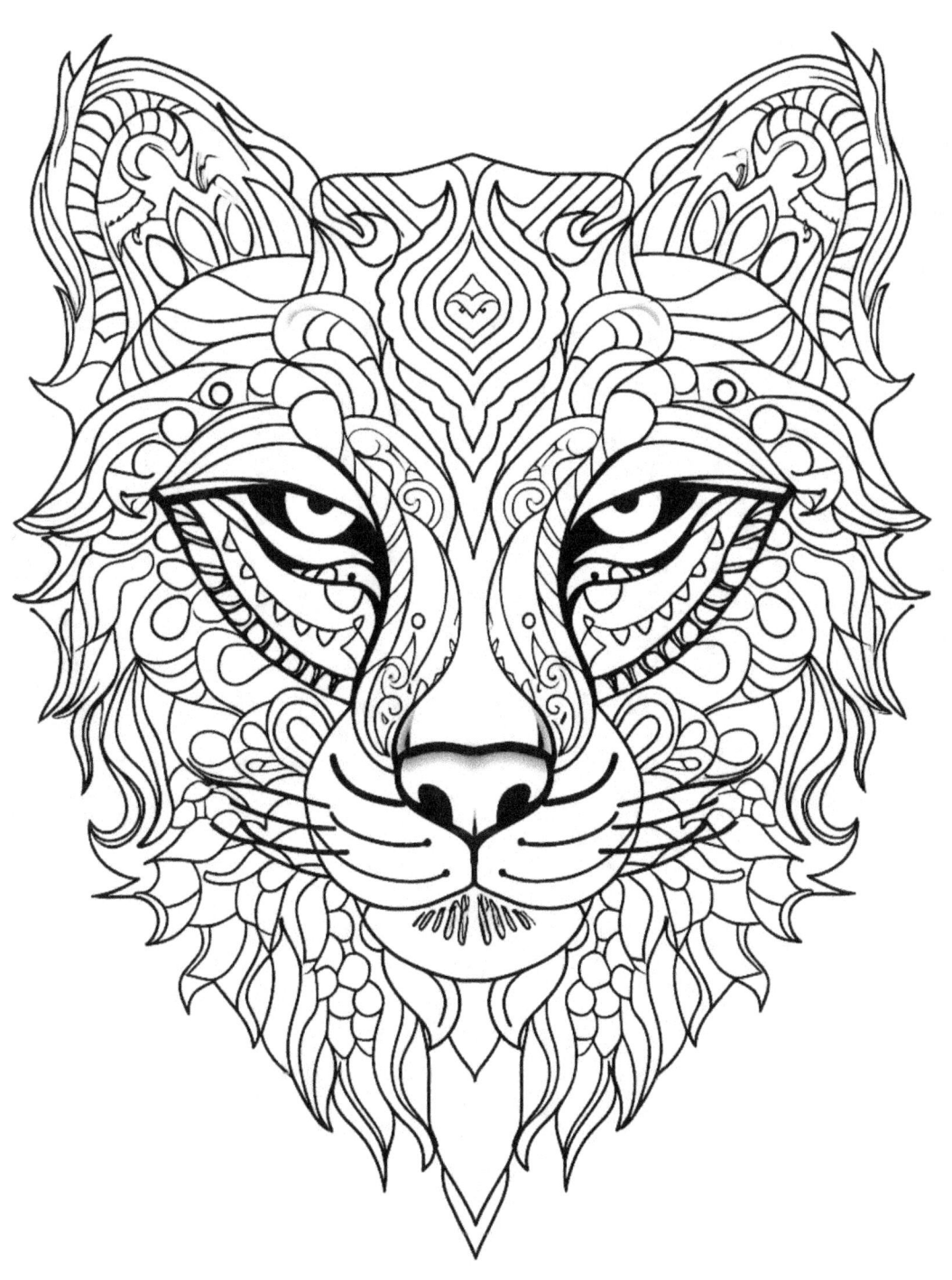

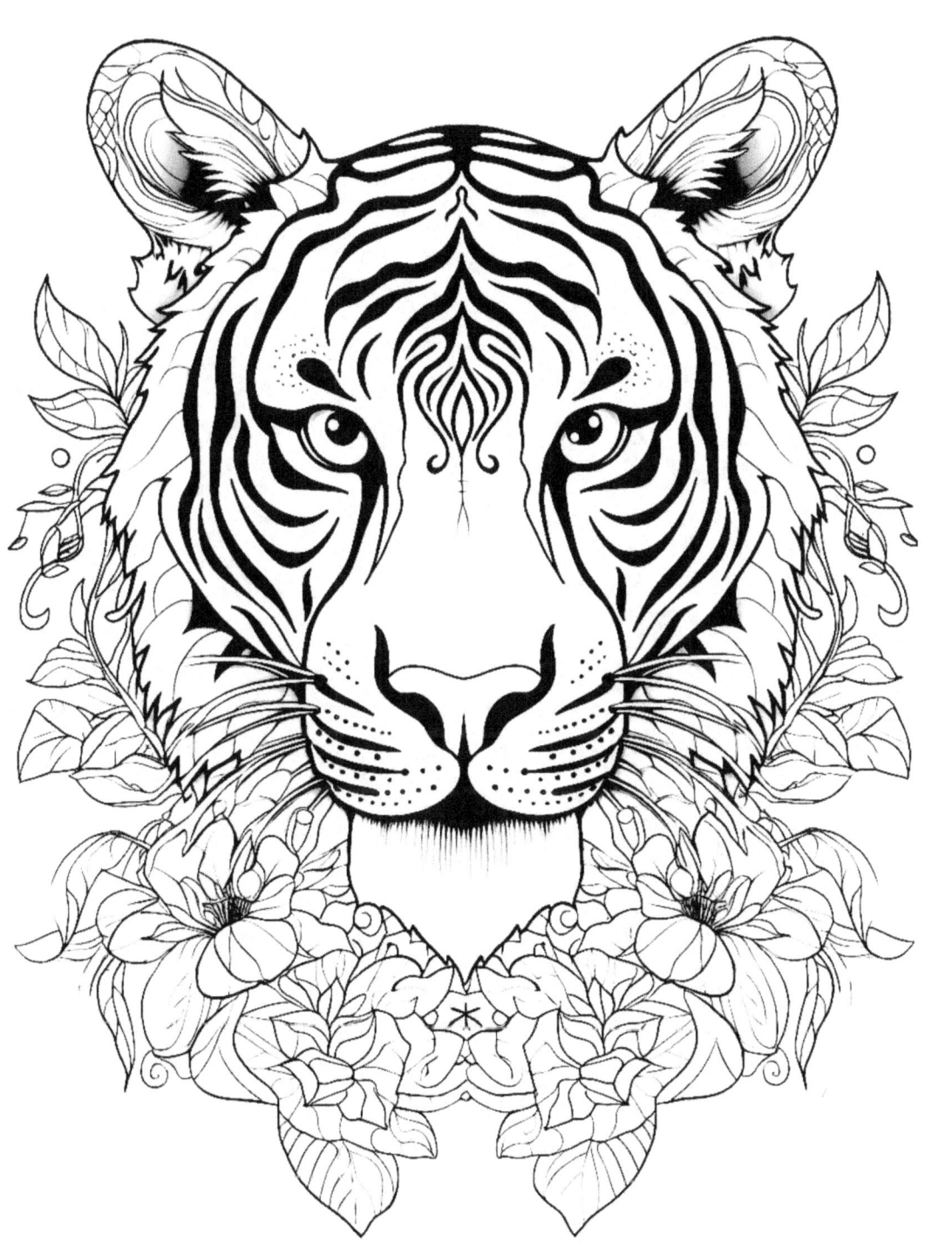

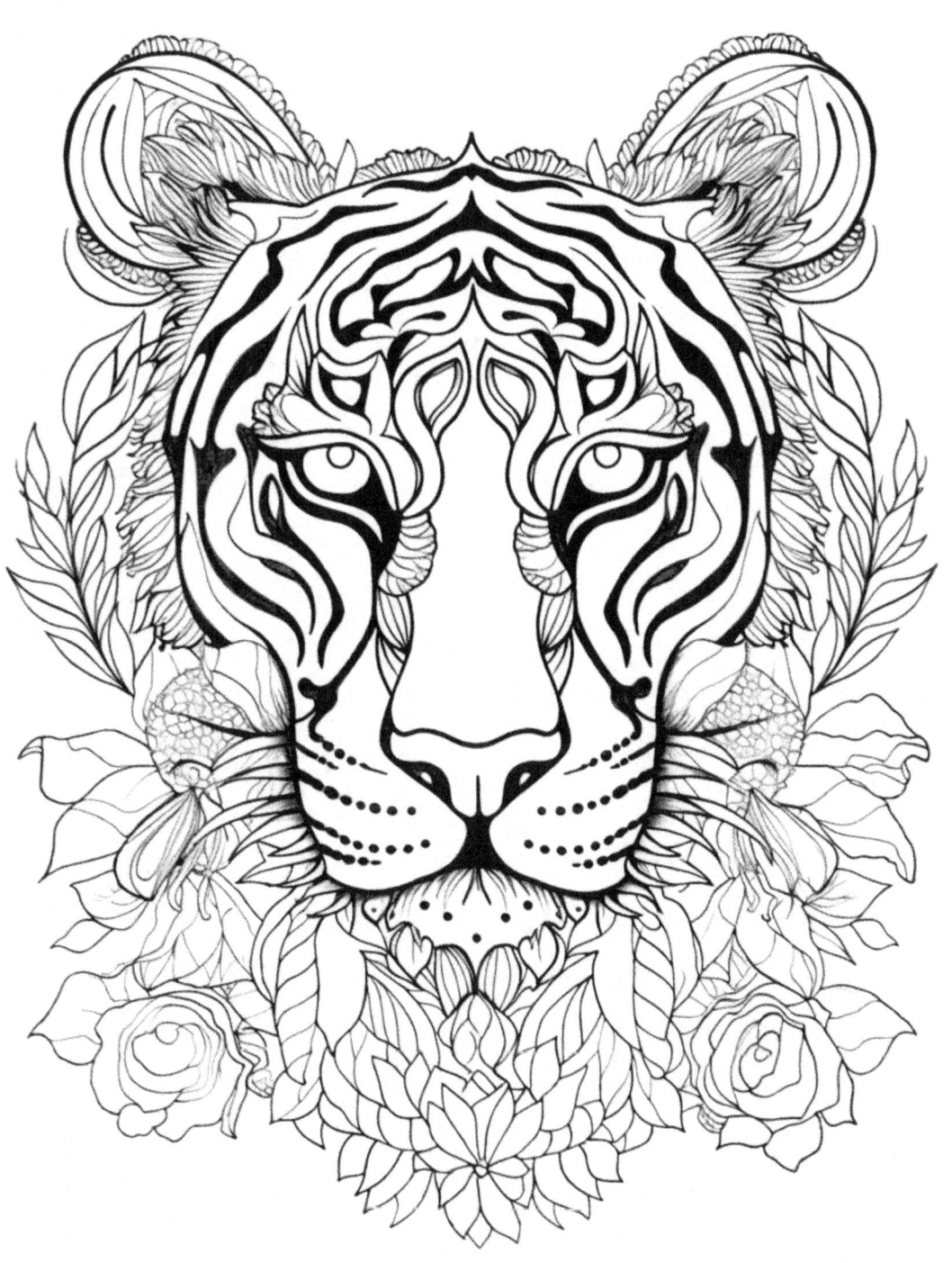

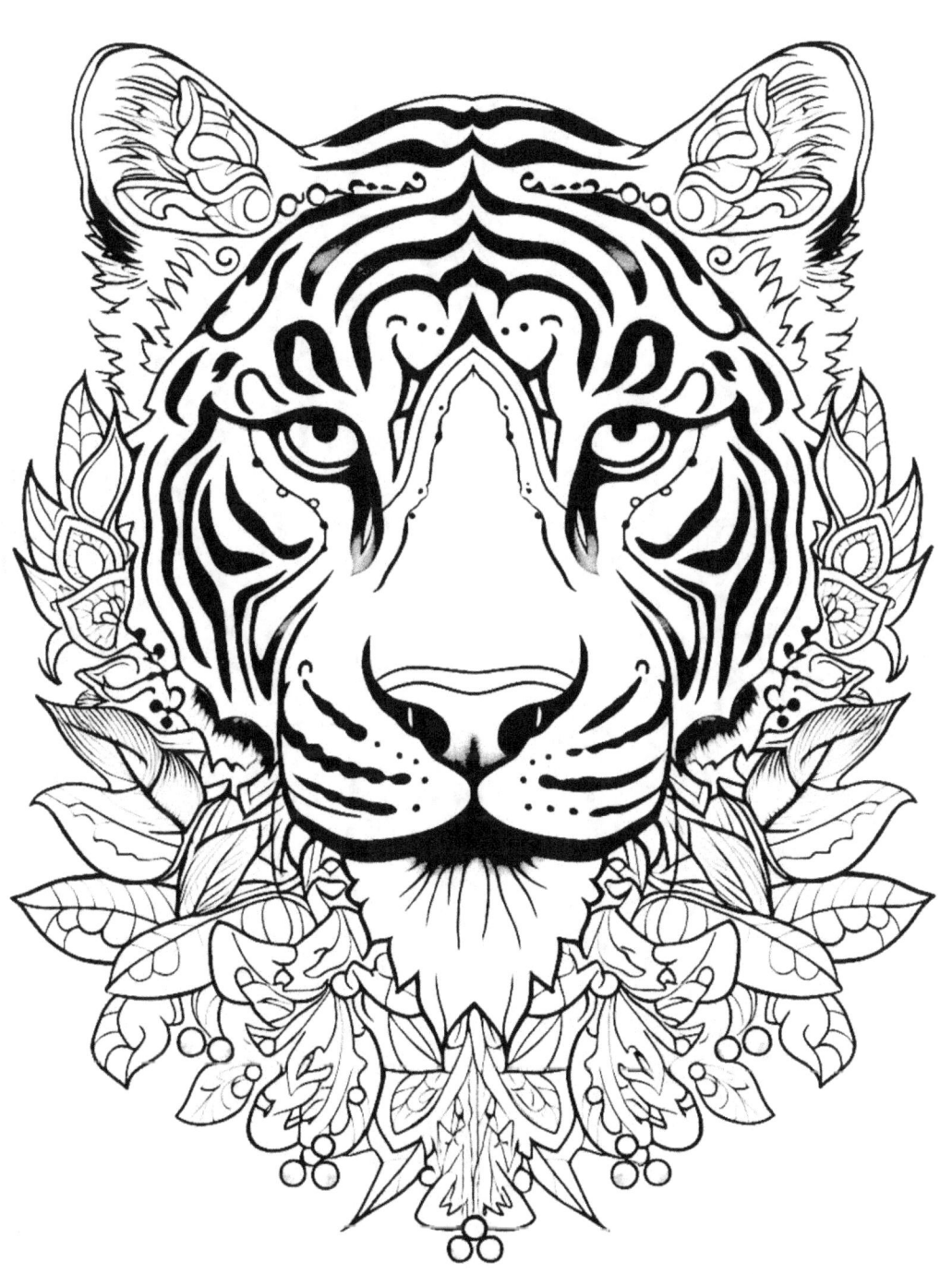

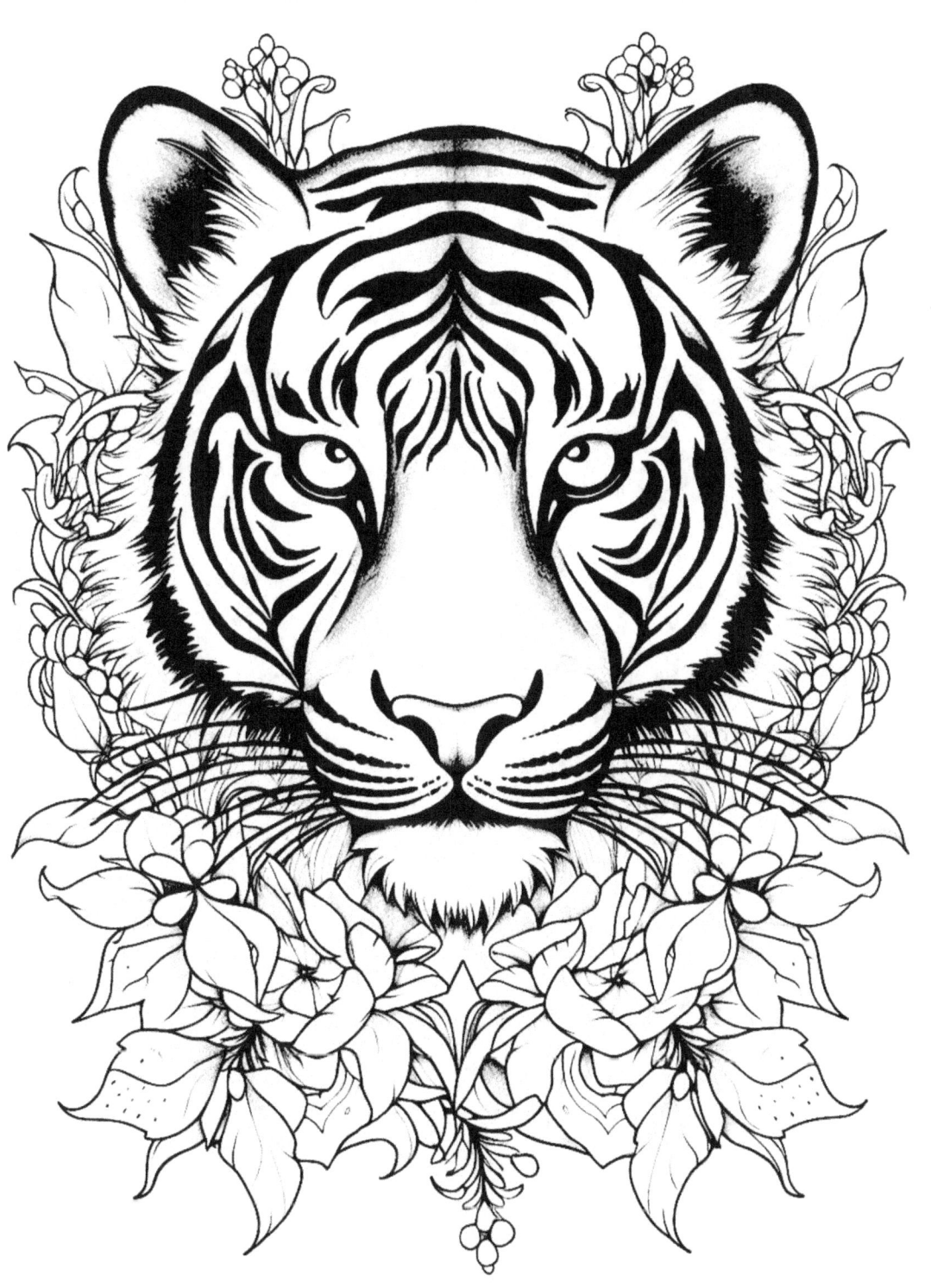

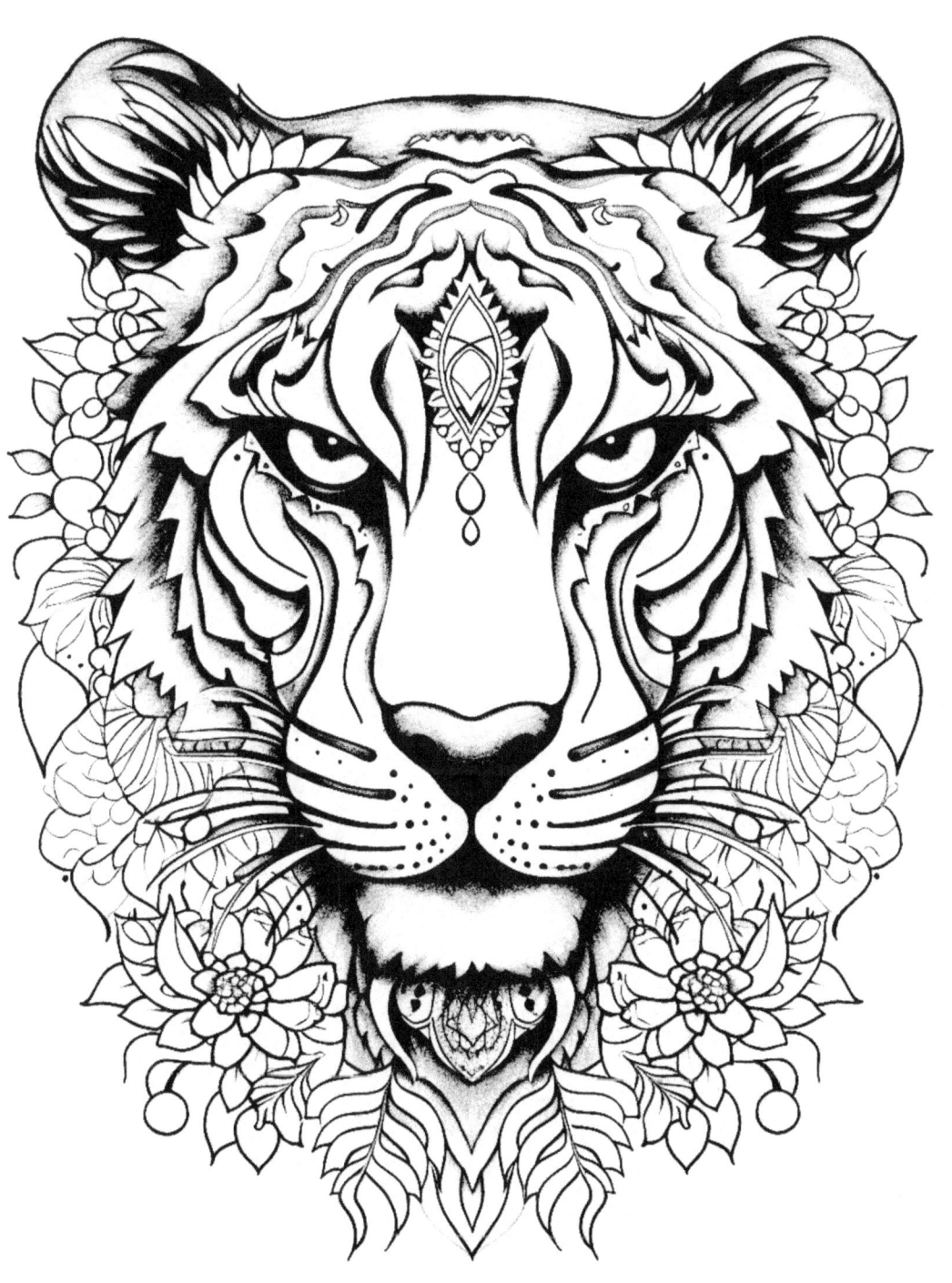

Panda

Meerkat

Dolphin

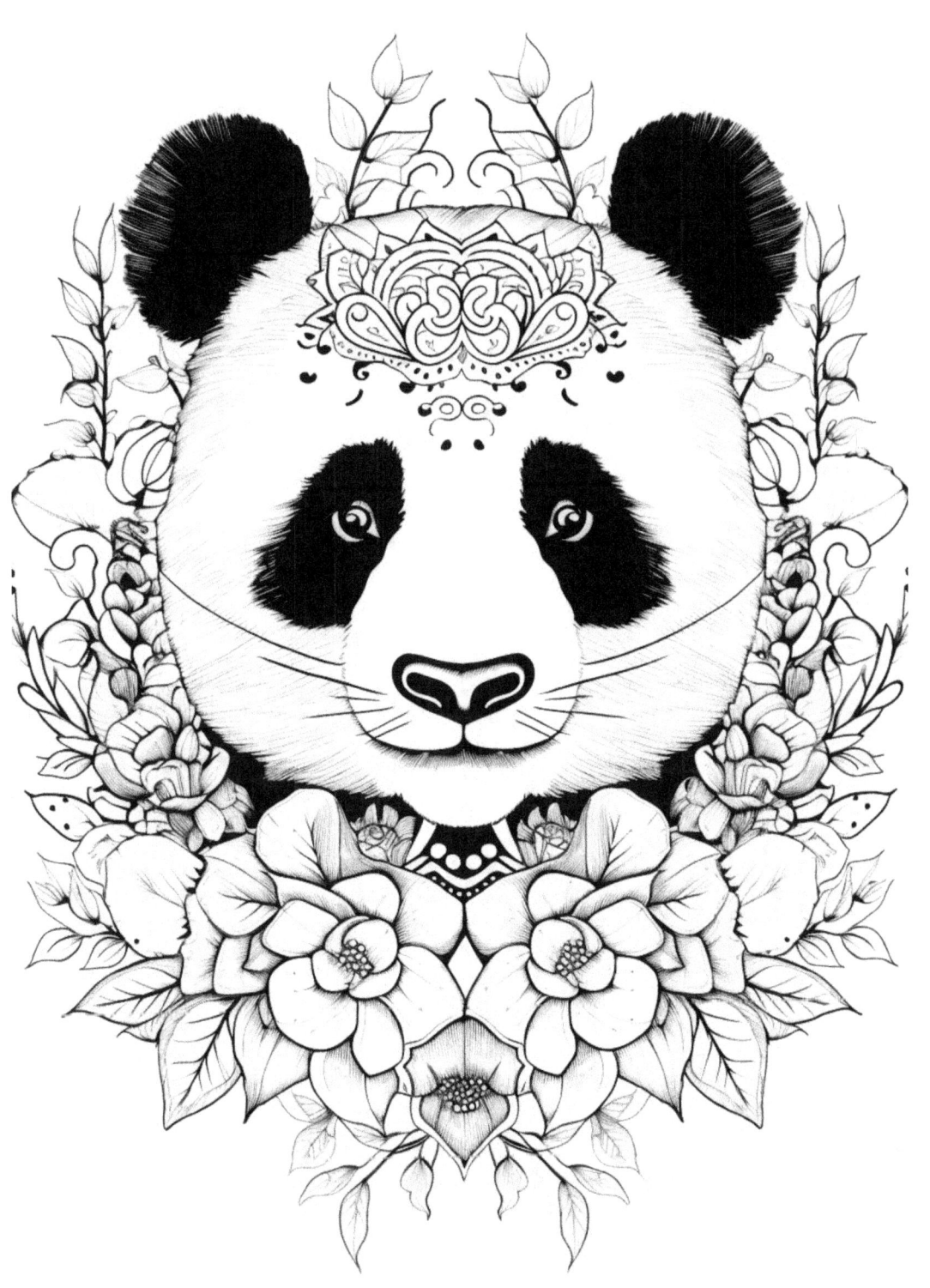

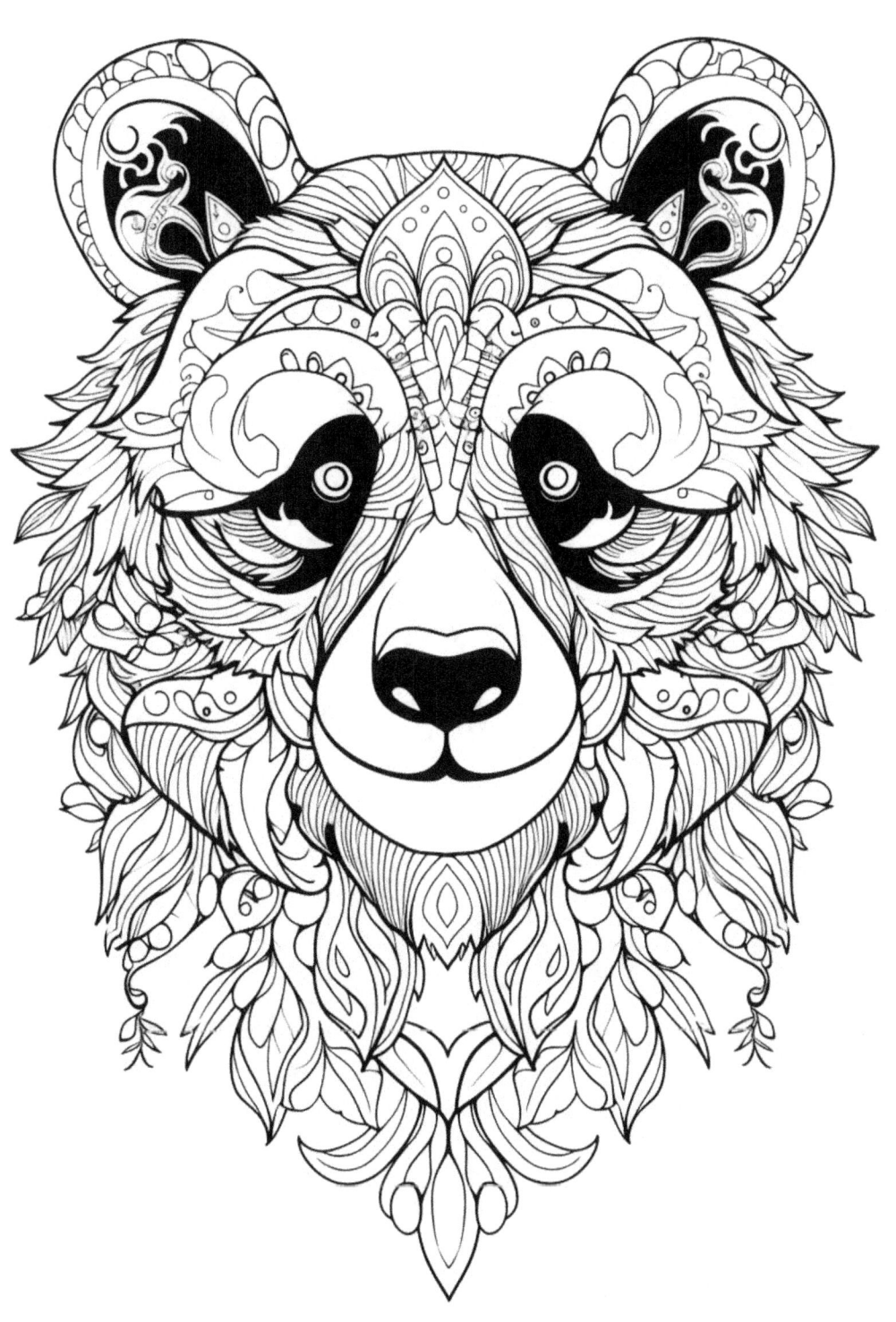

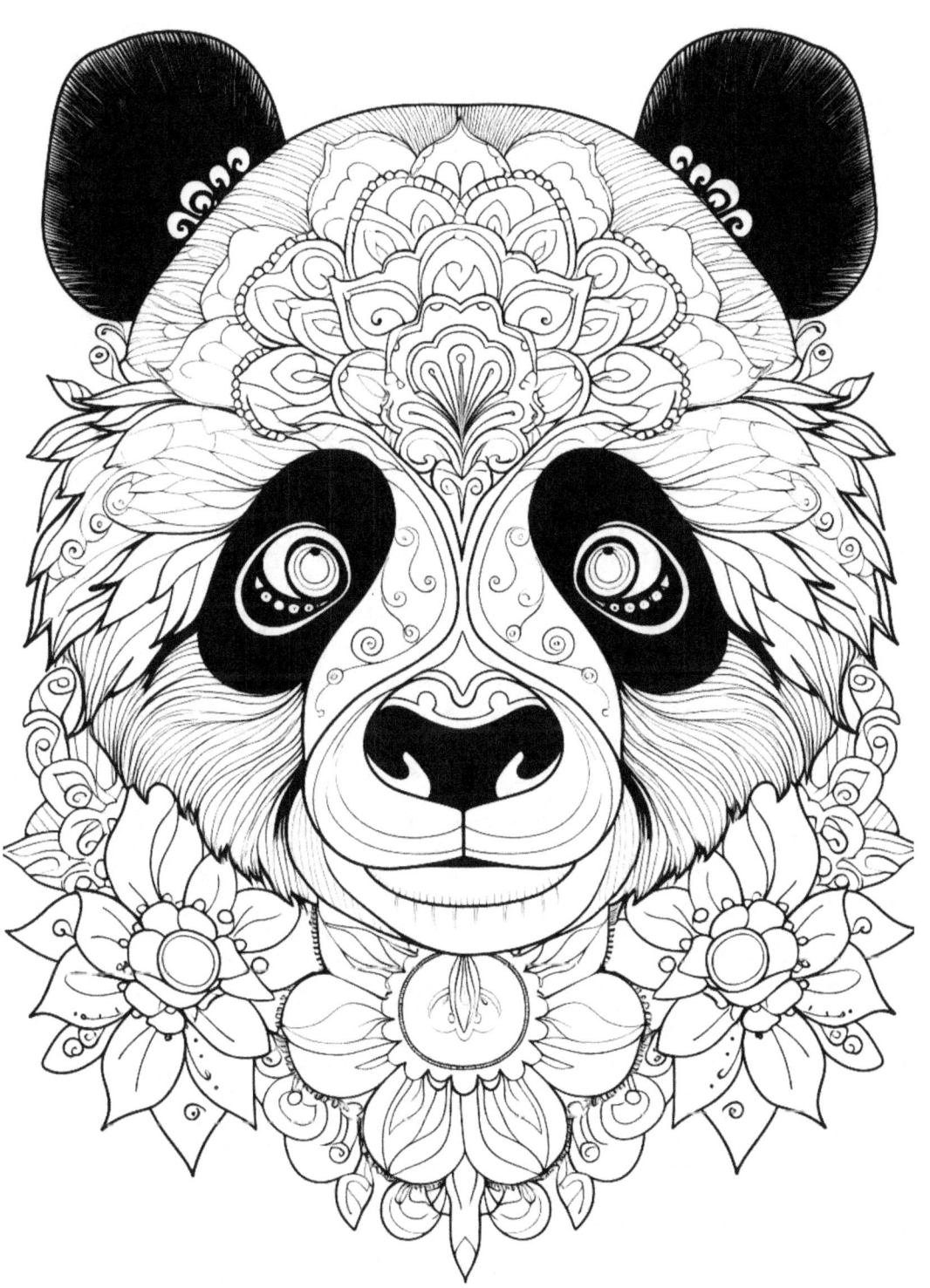

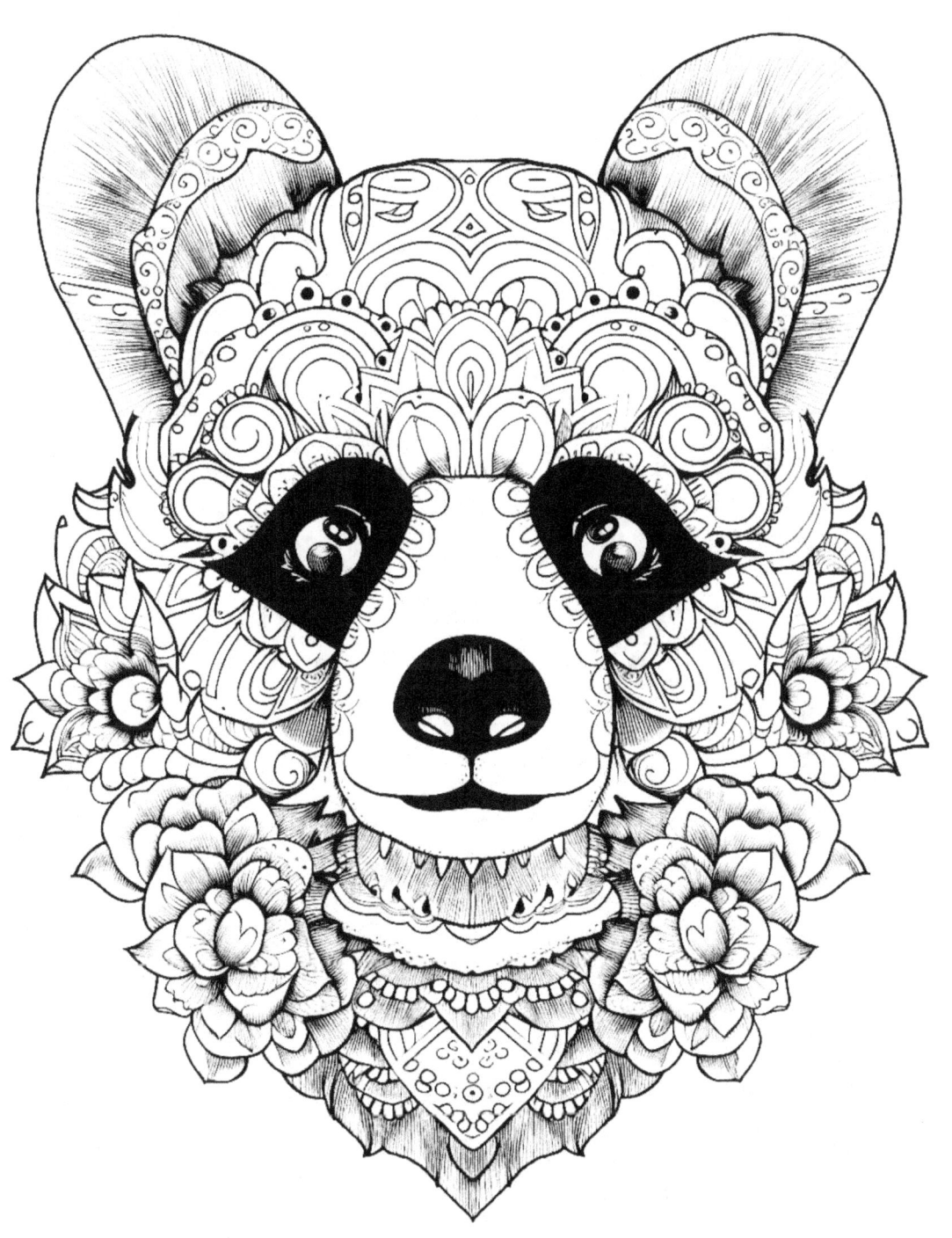

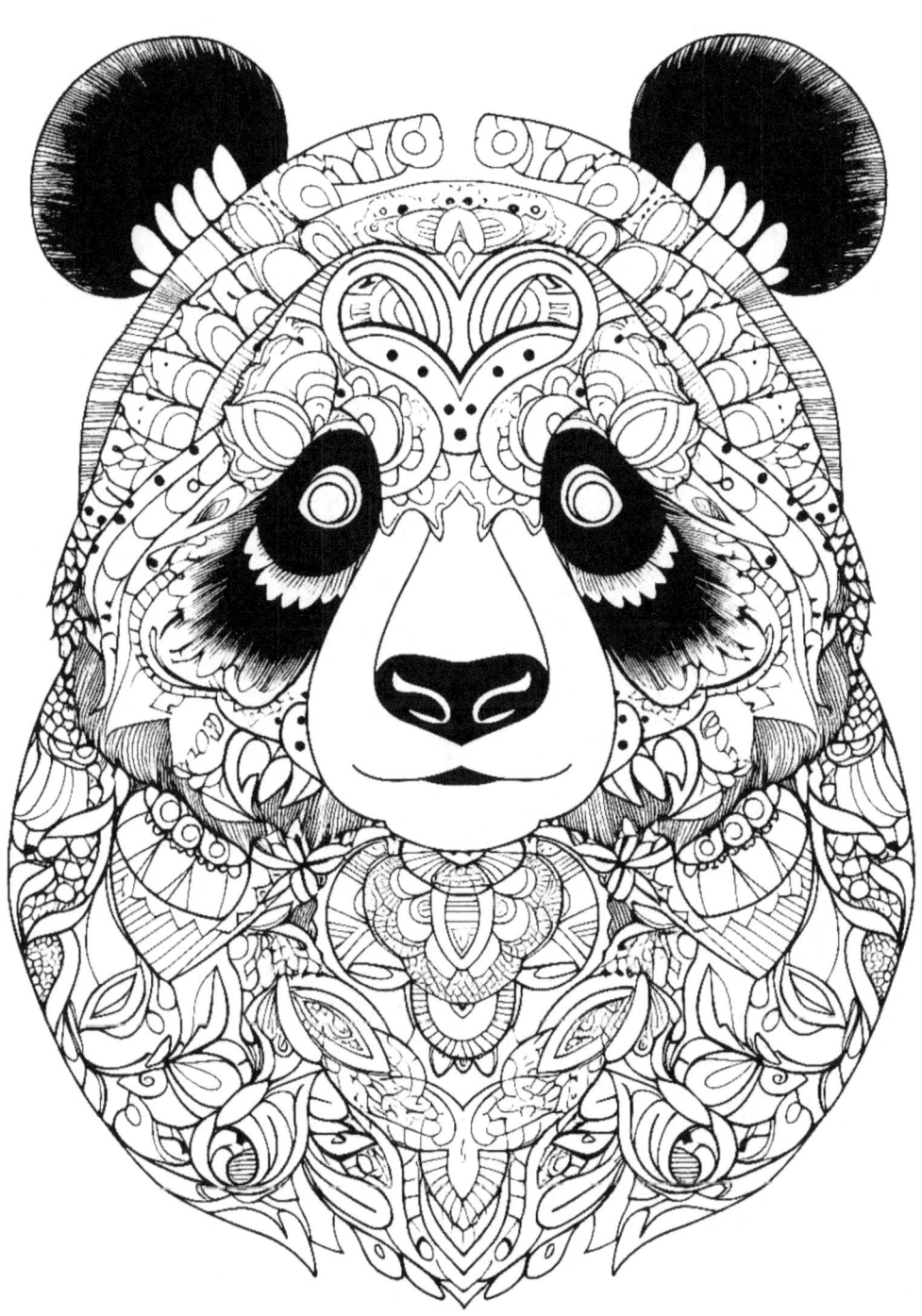

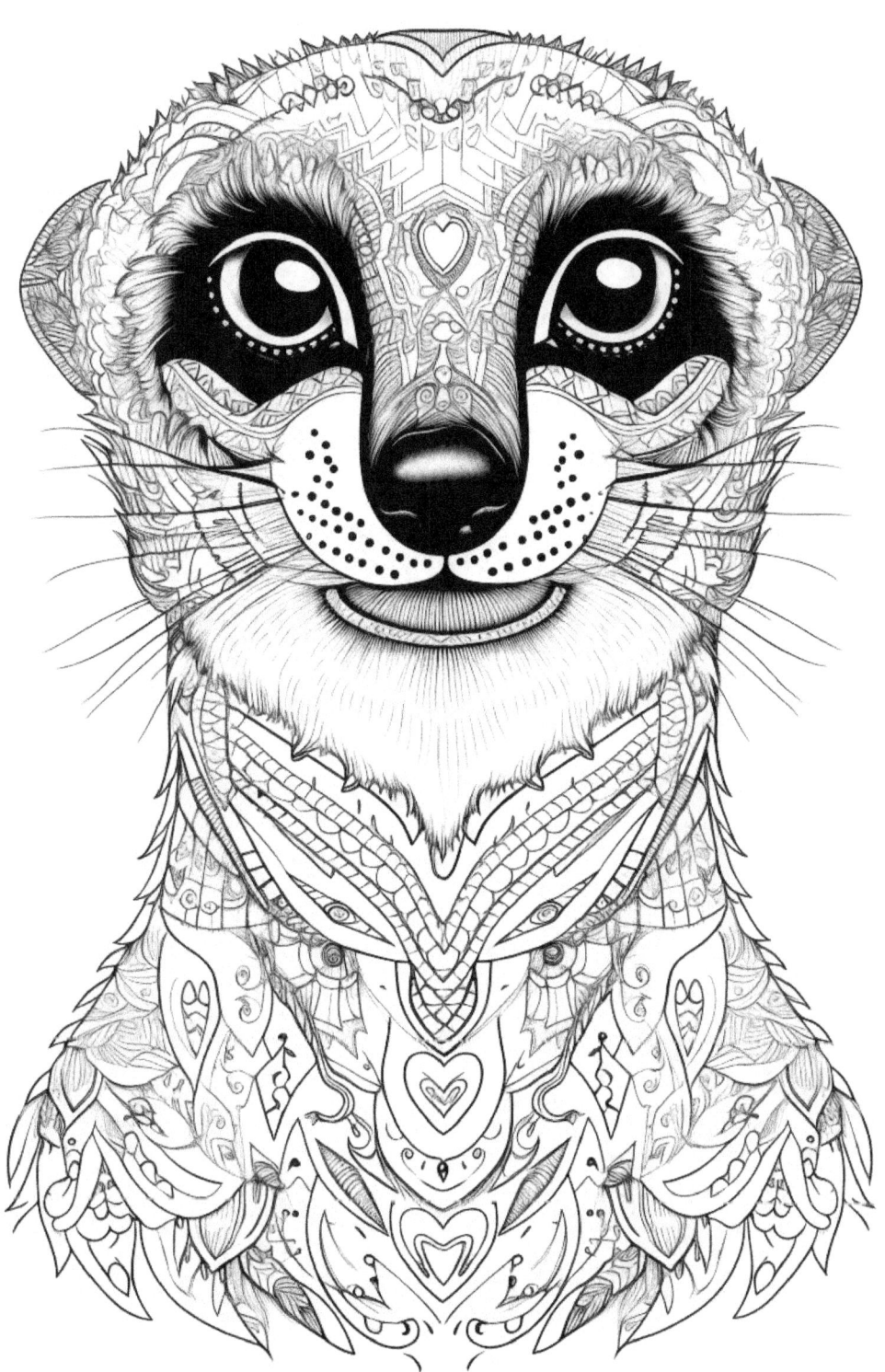

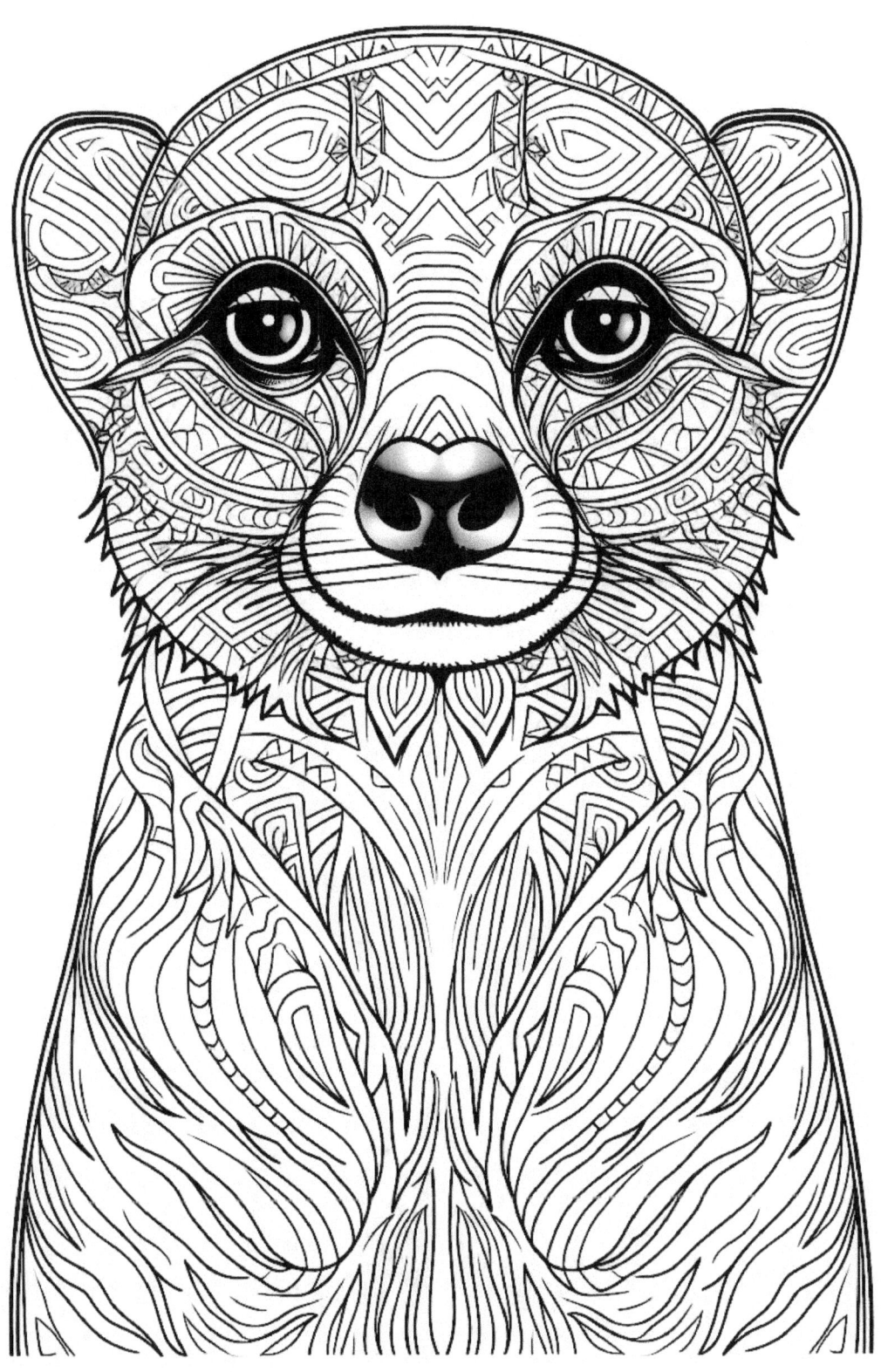

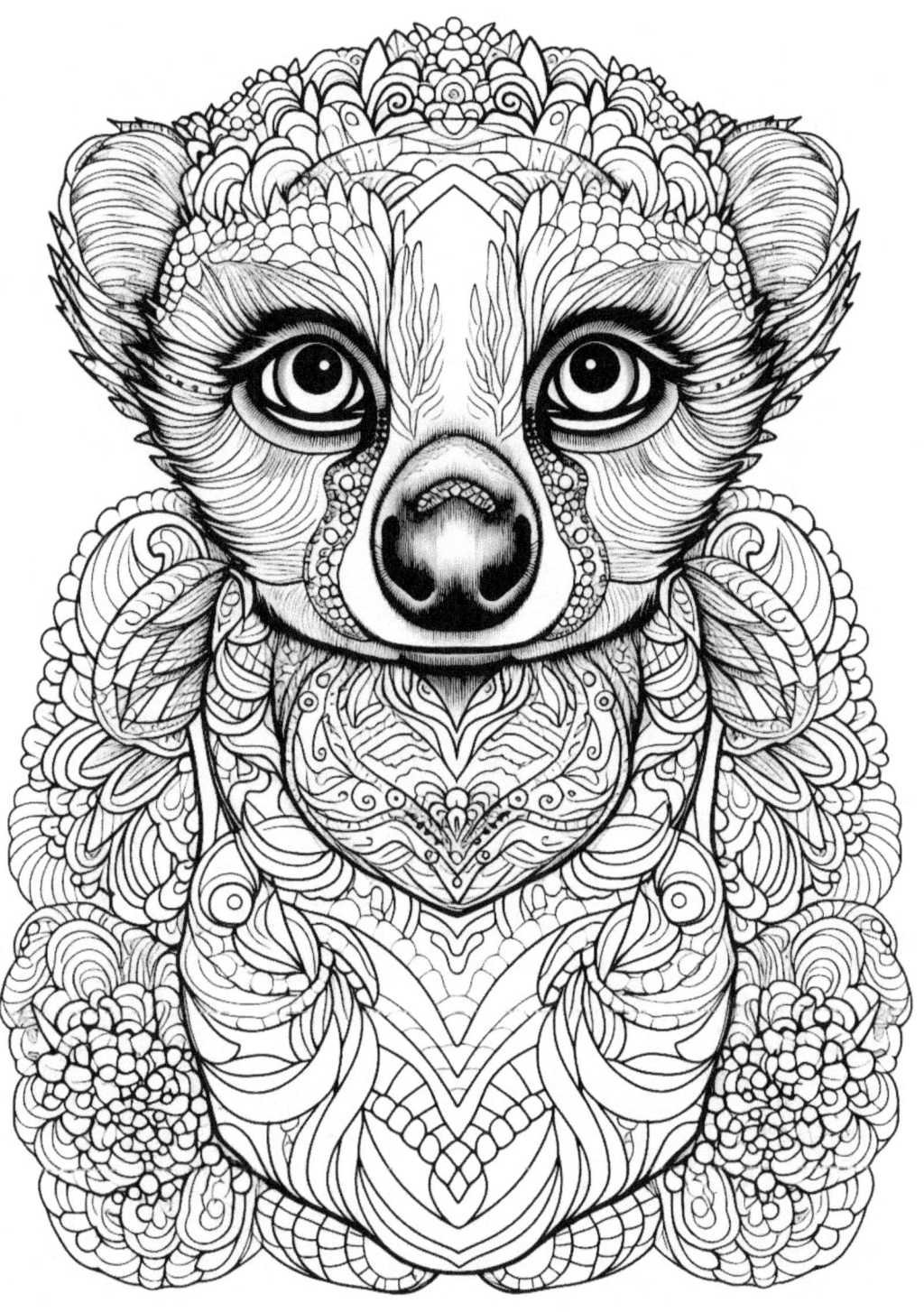

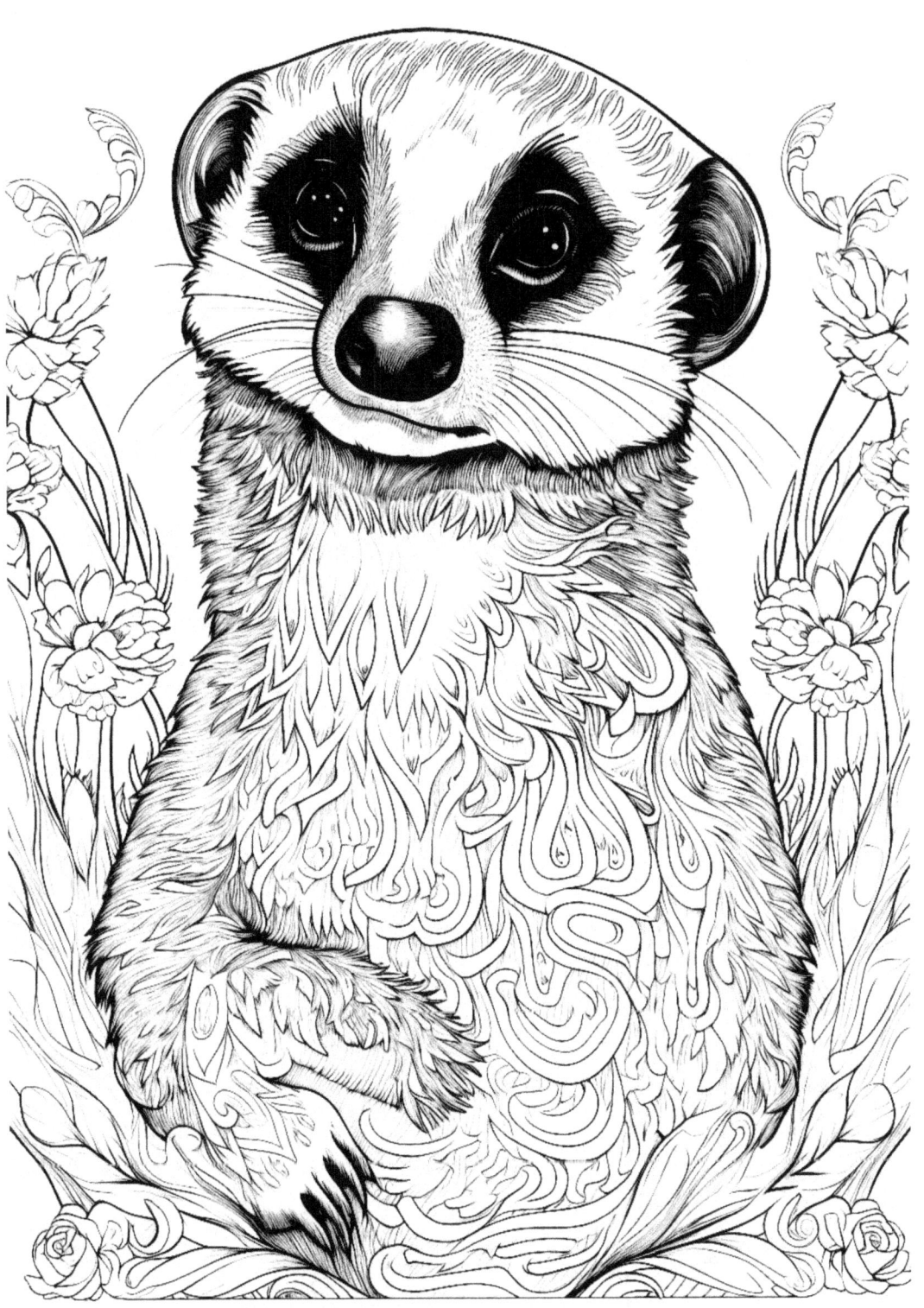

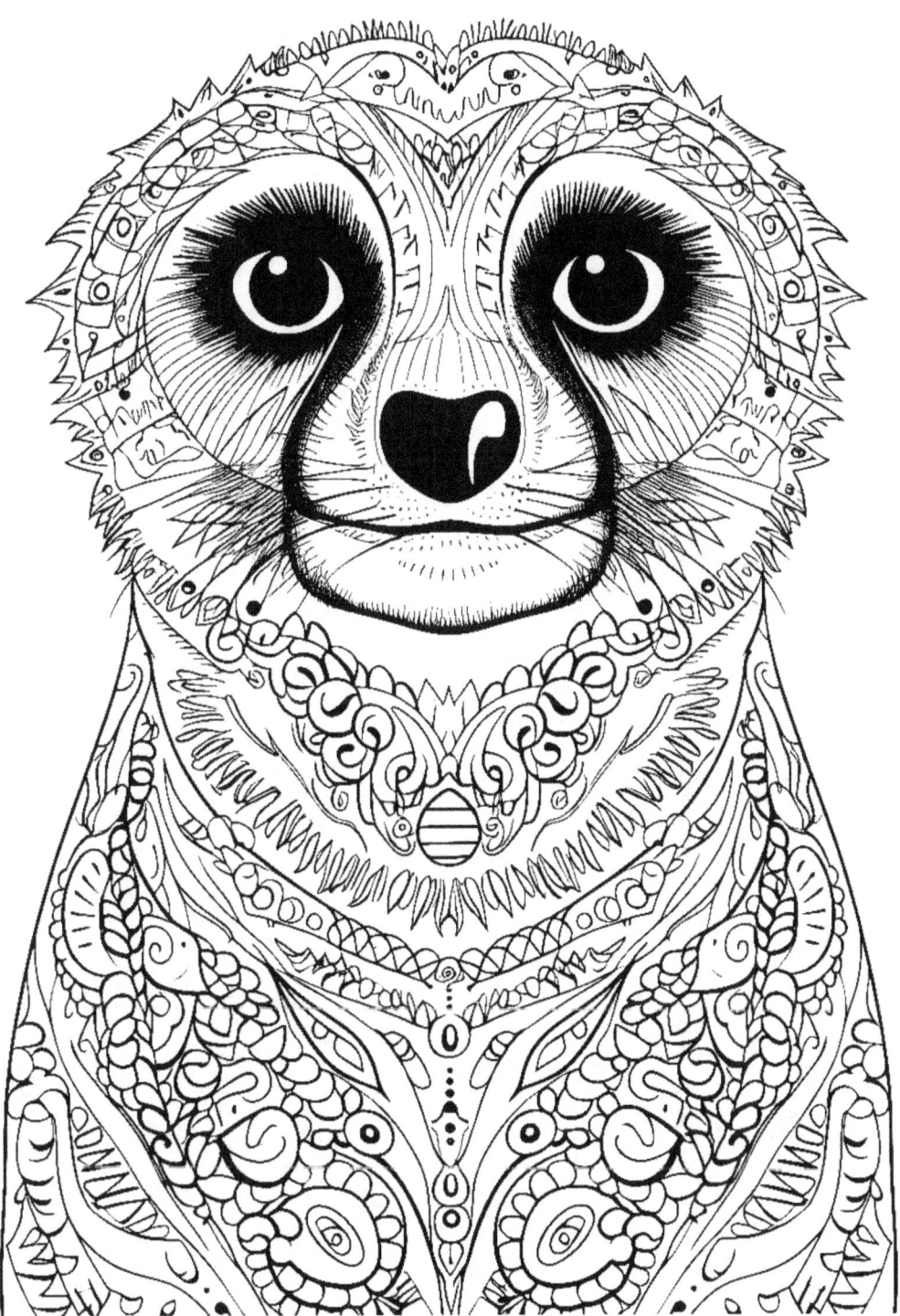

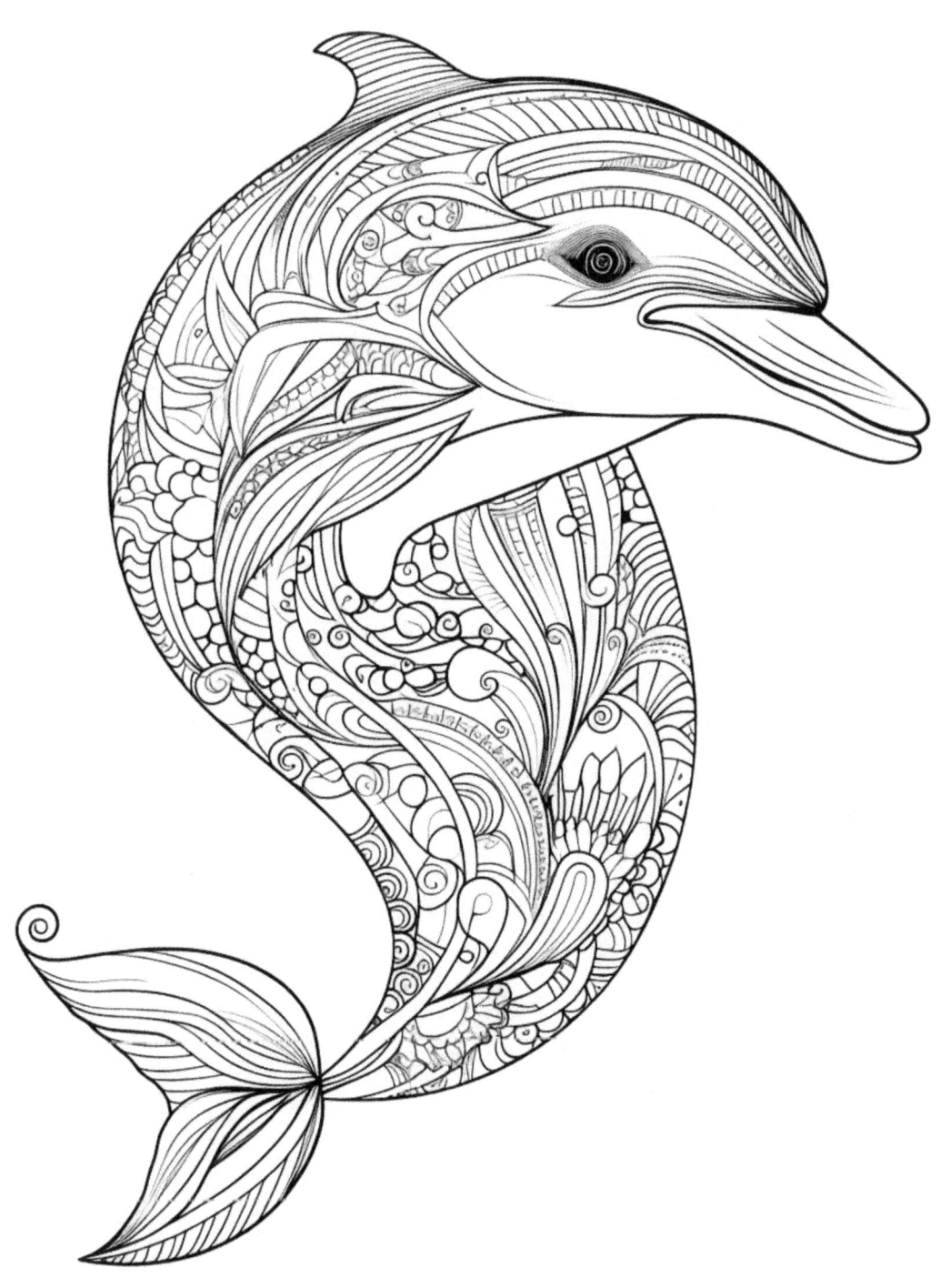

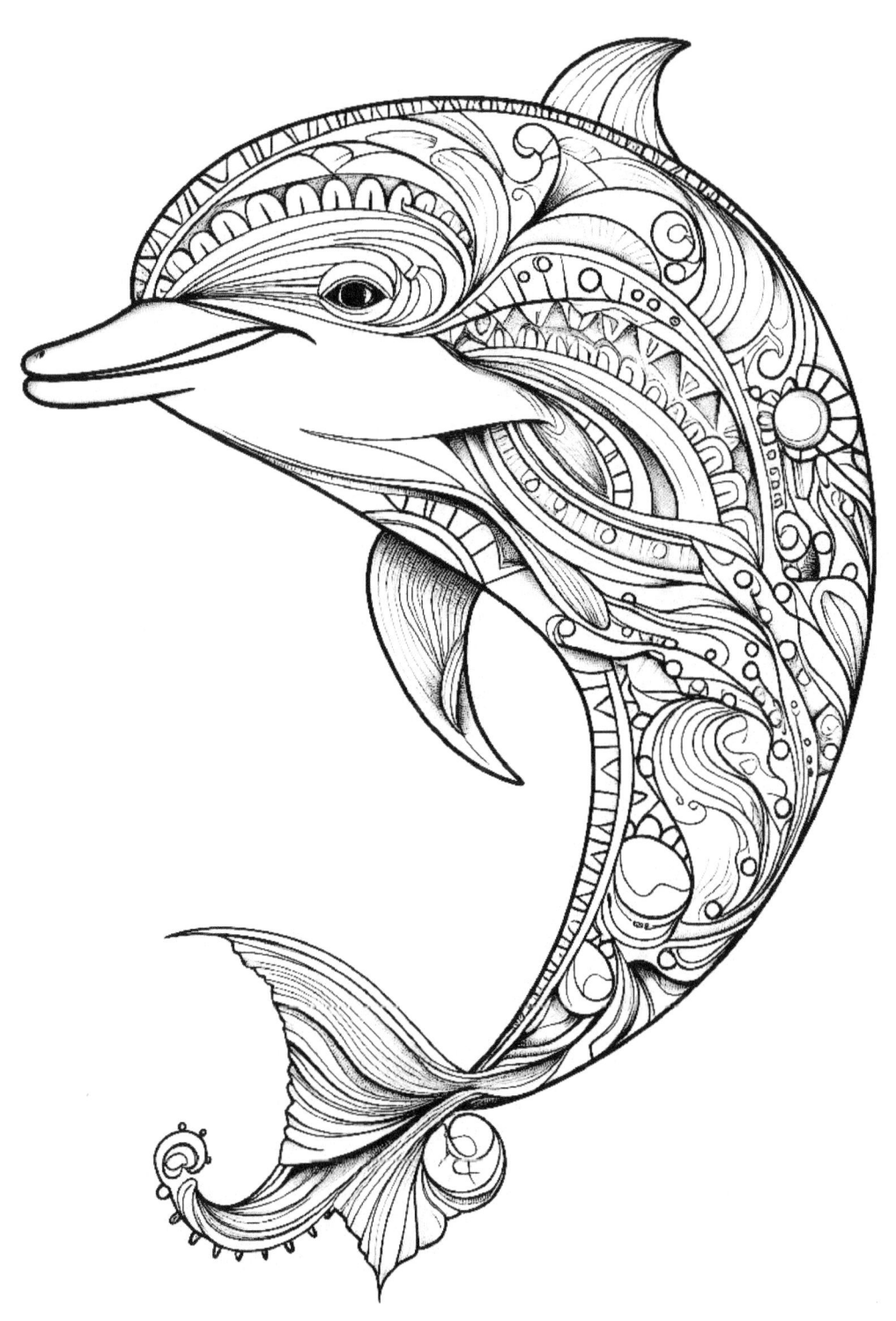

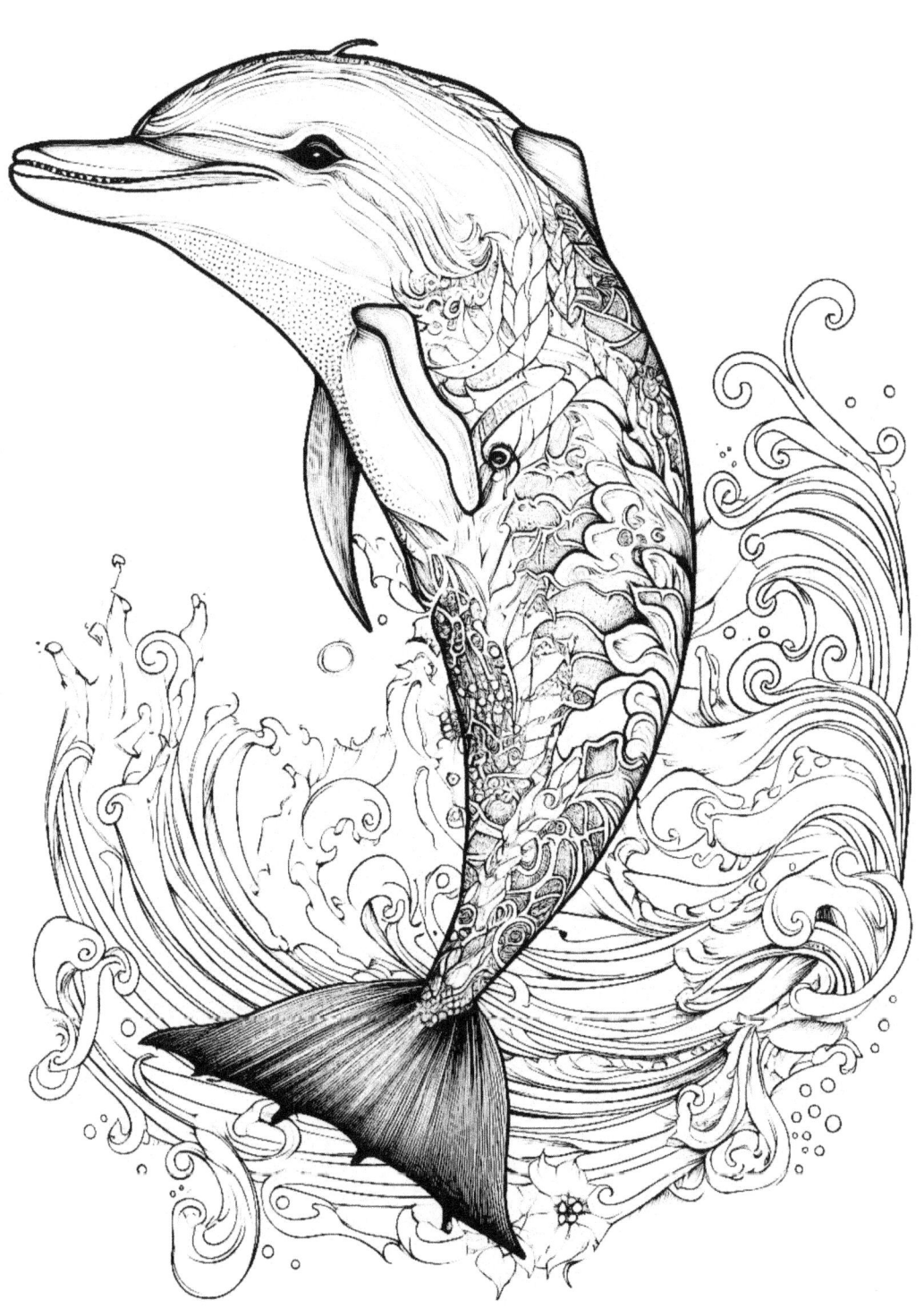

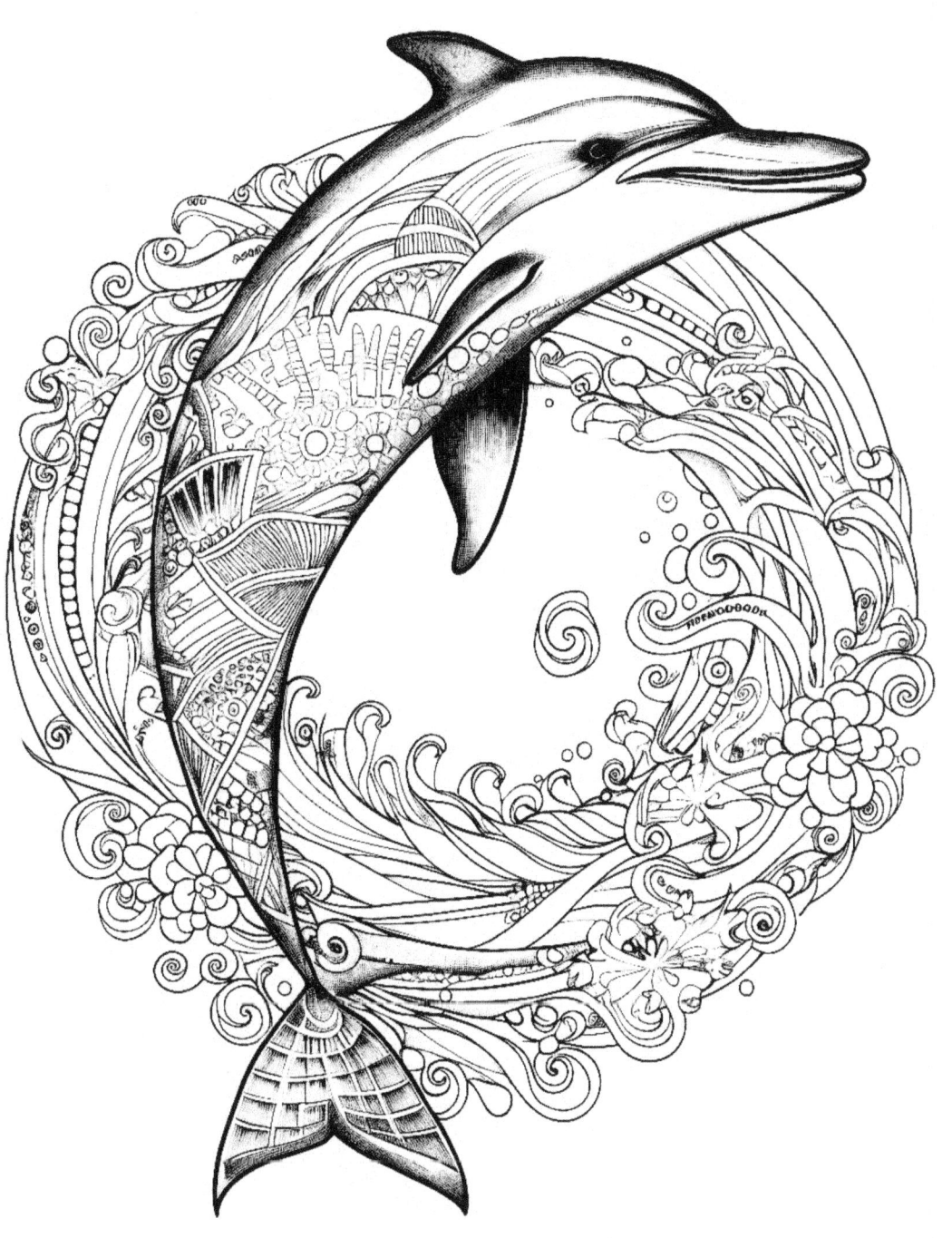

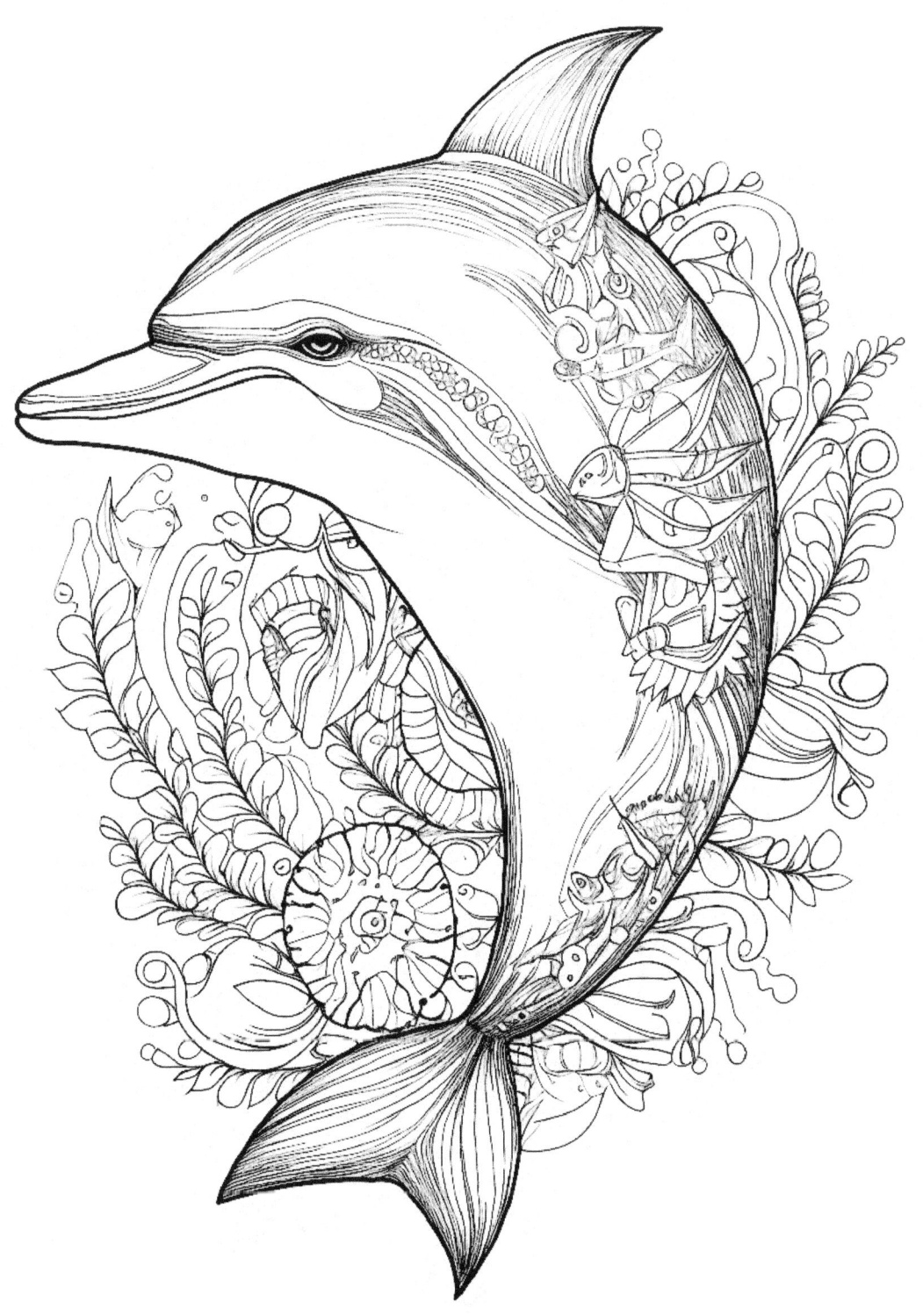

Zebra

Elephant

Giraffe

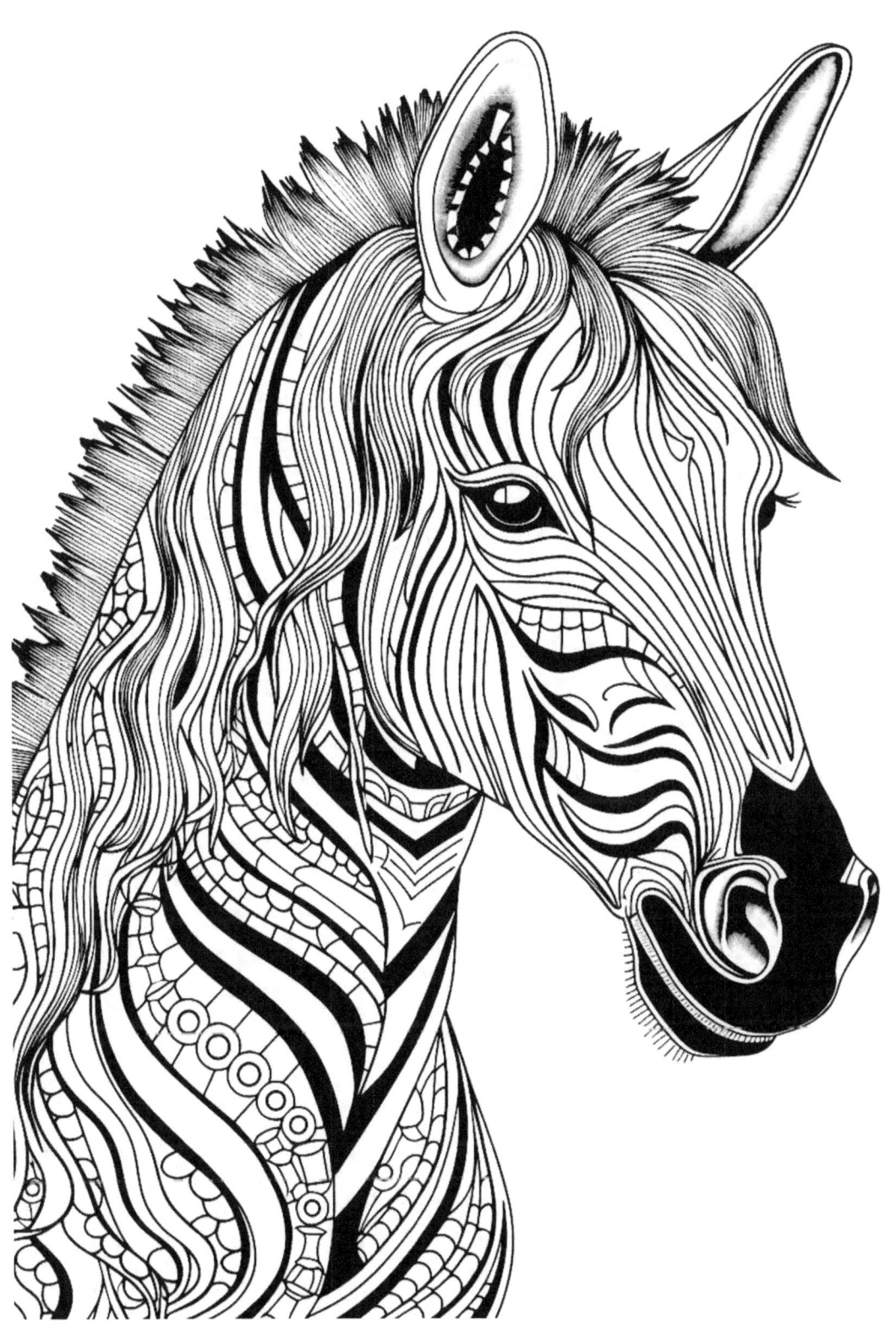

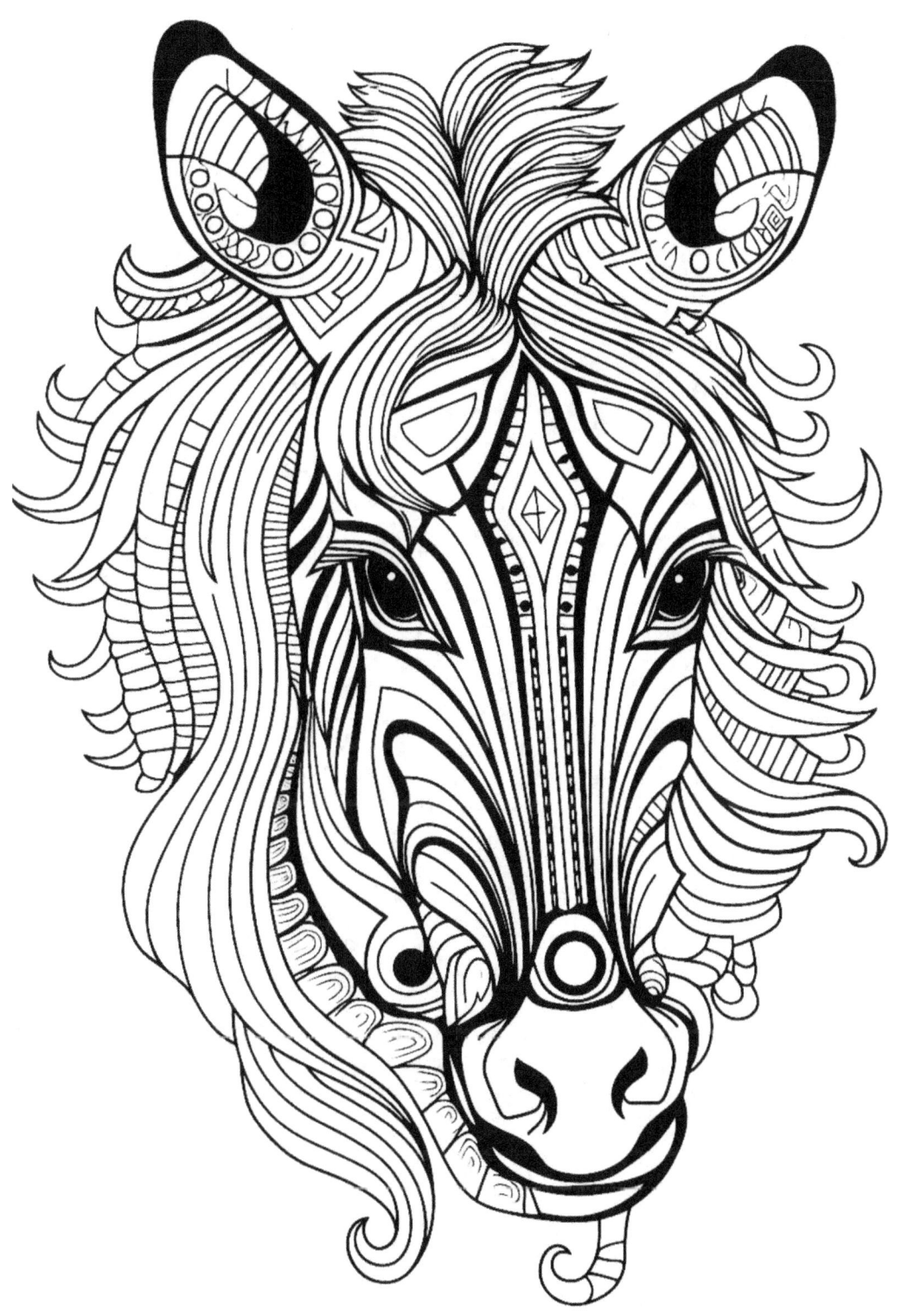

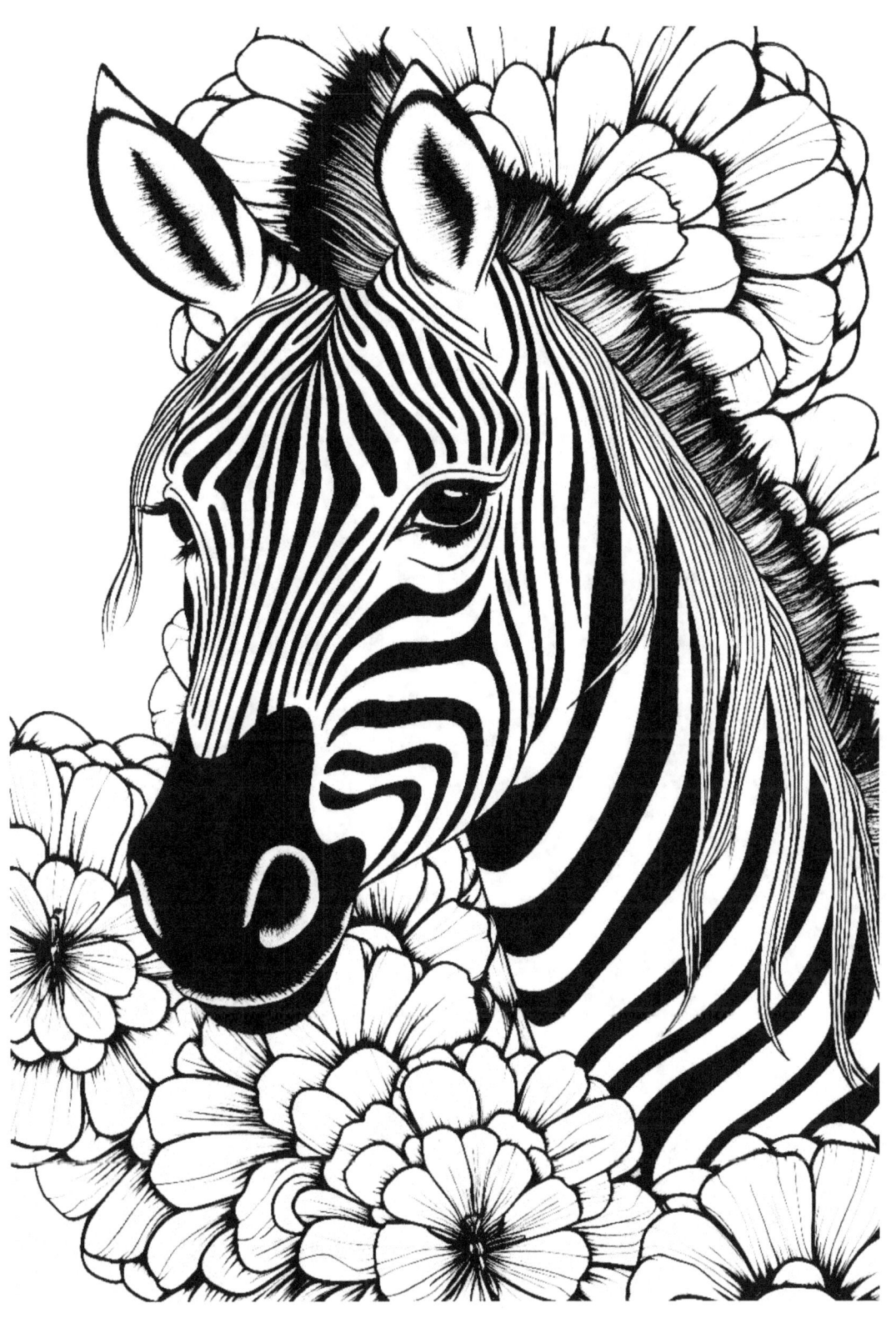

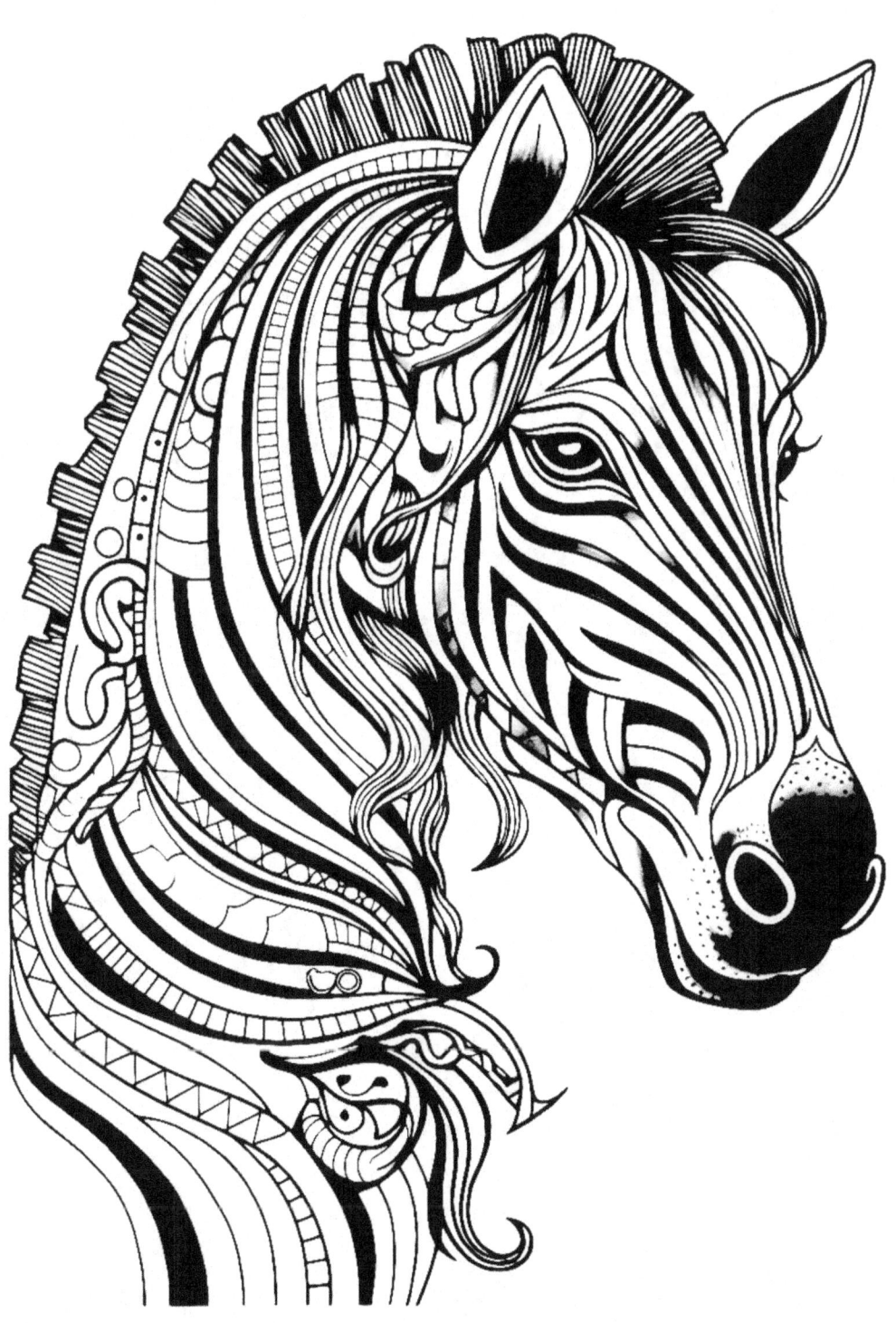

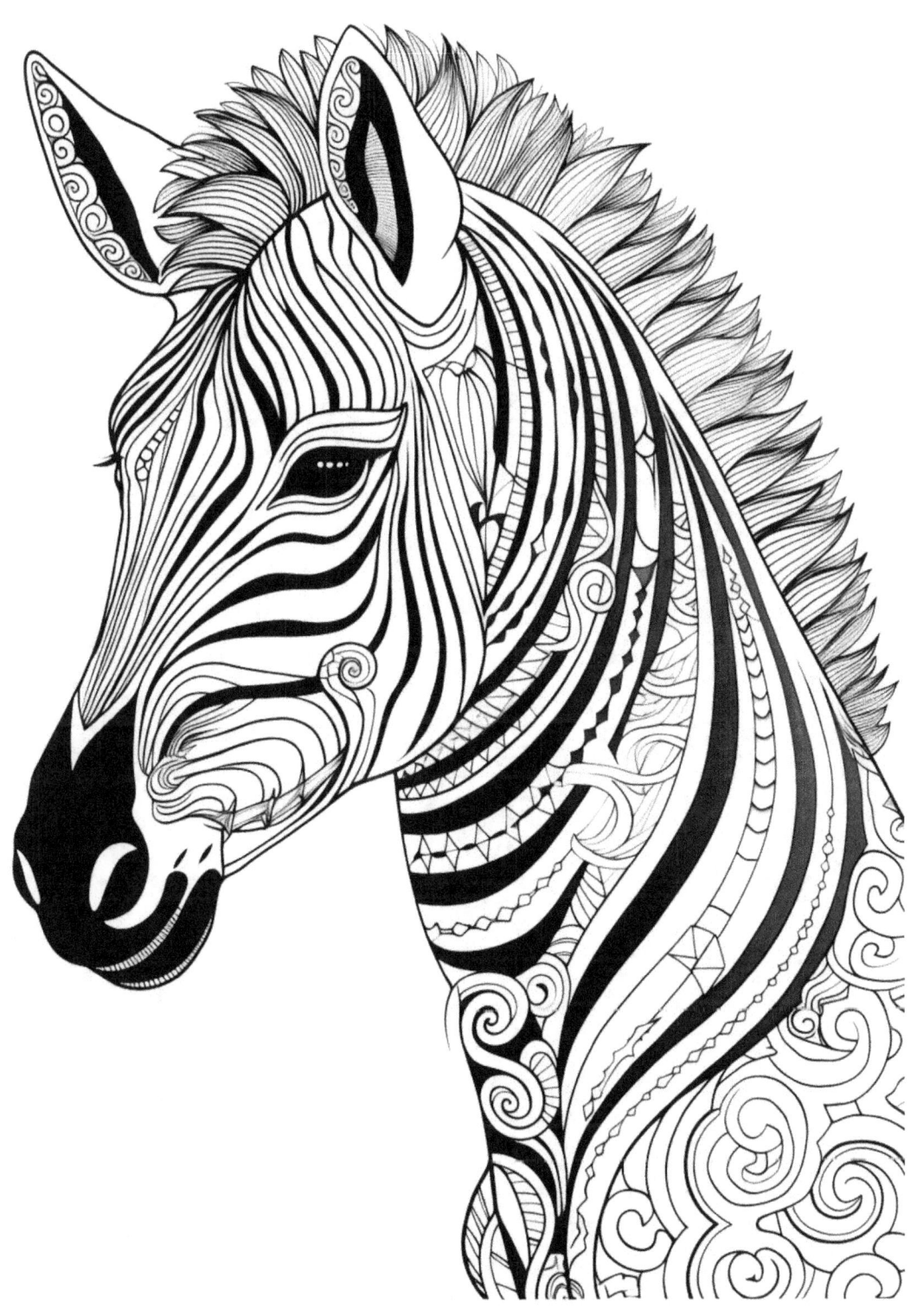

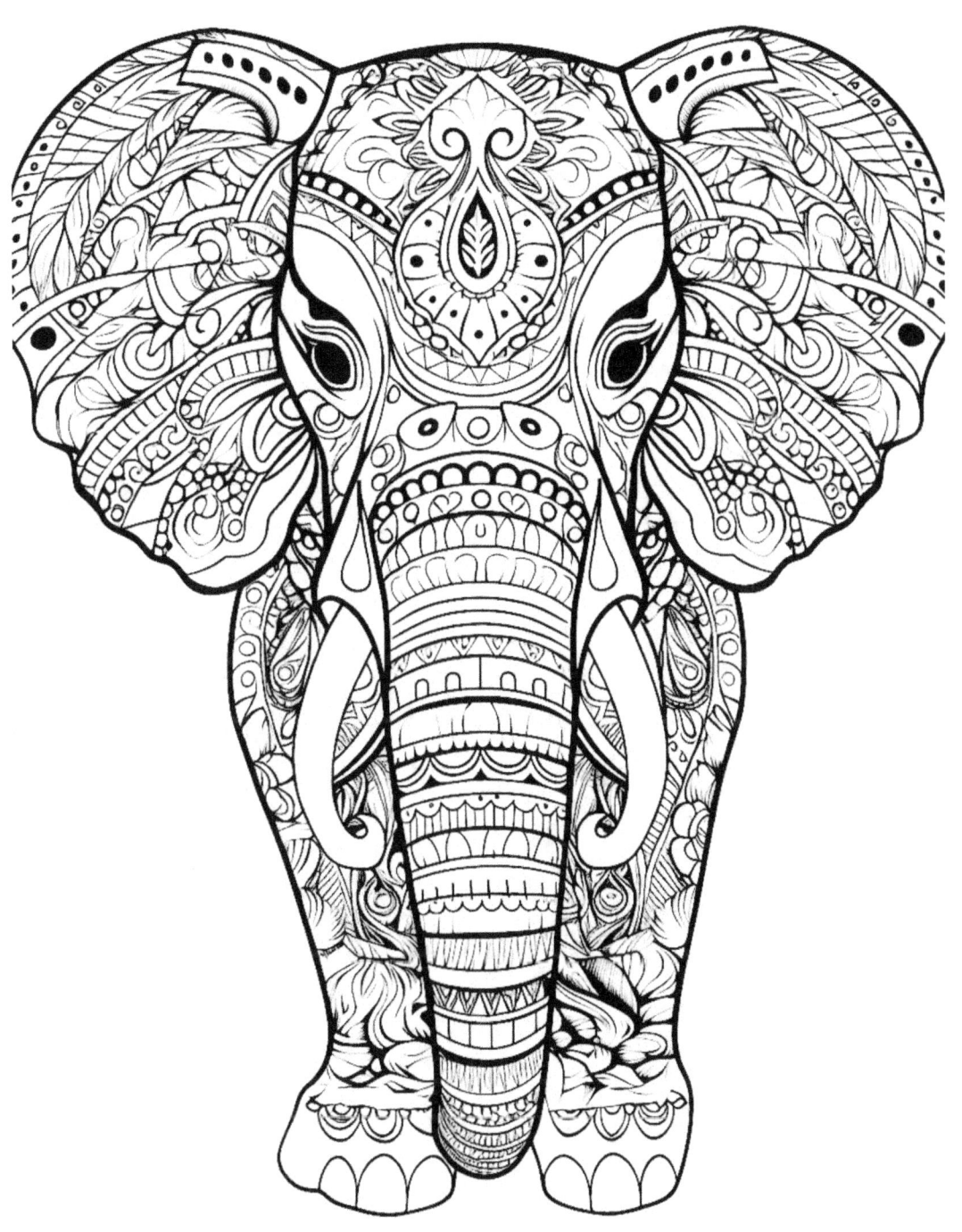

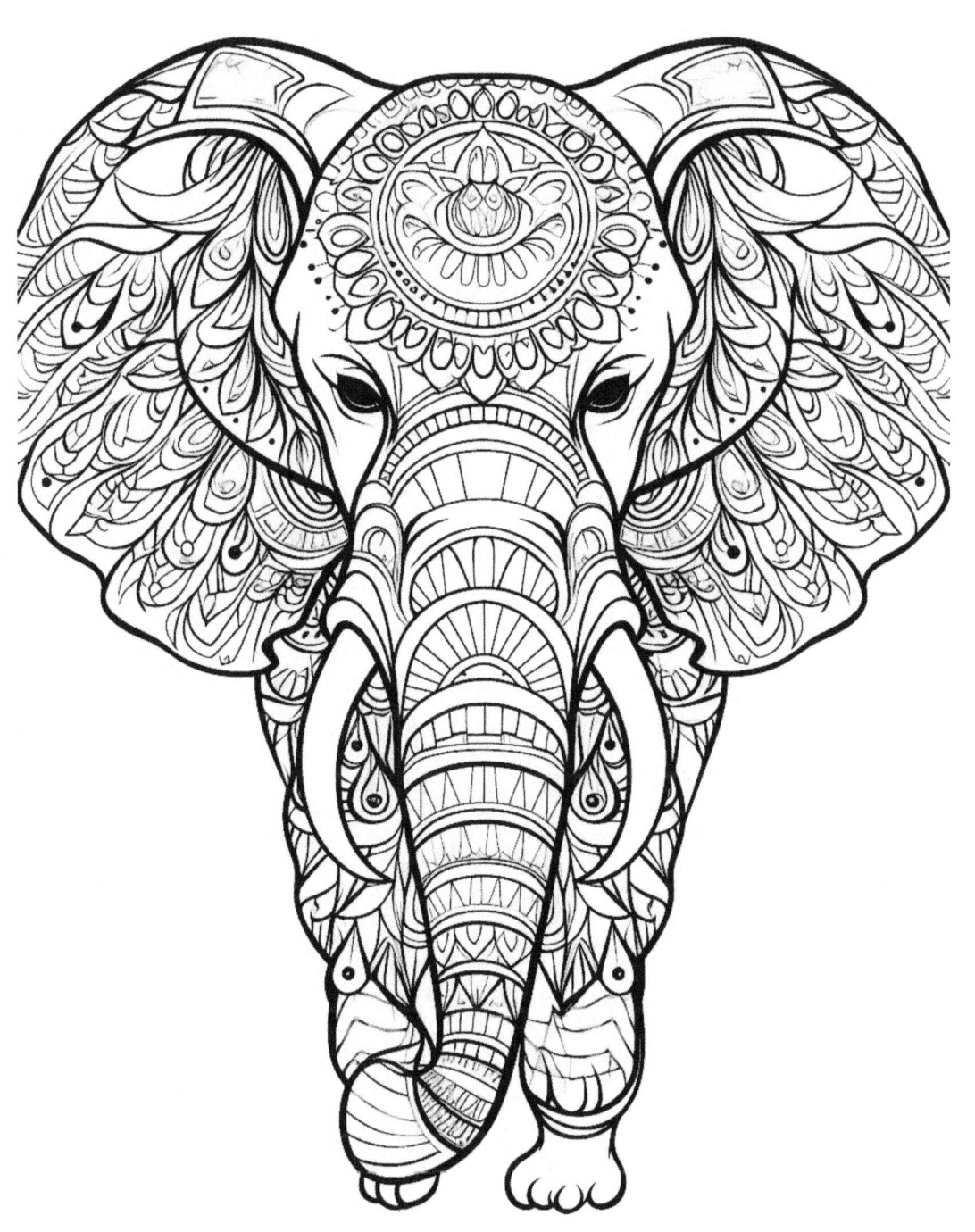

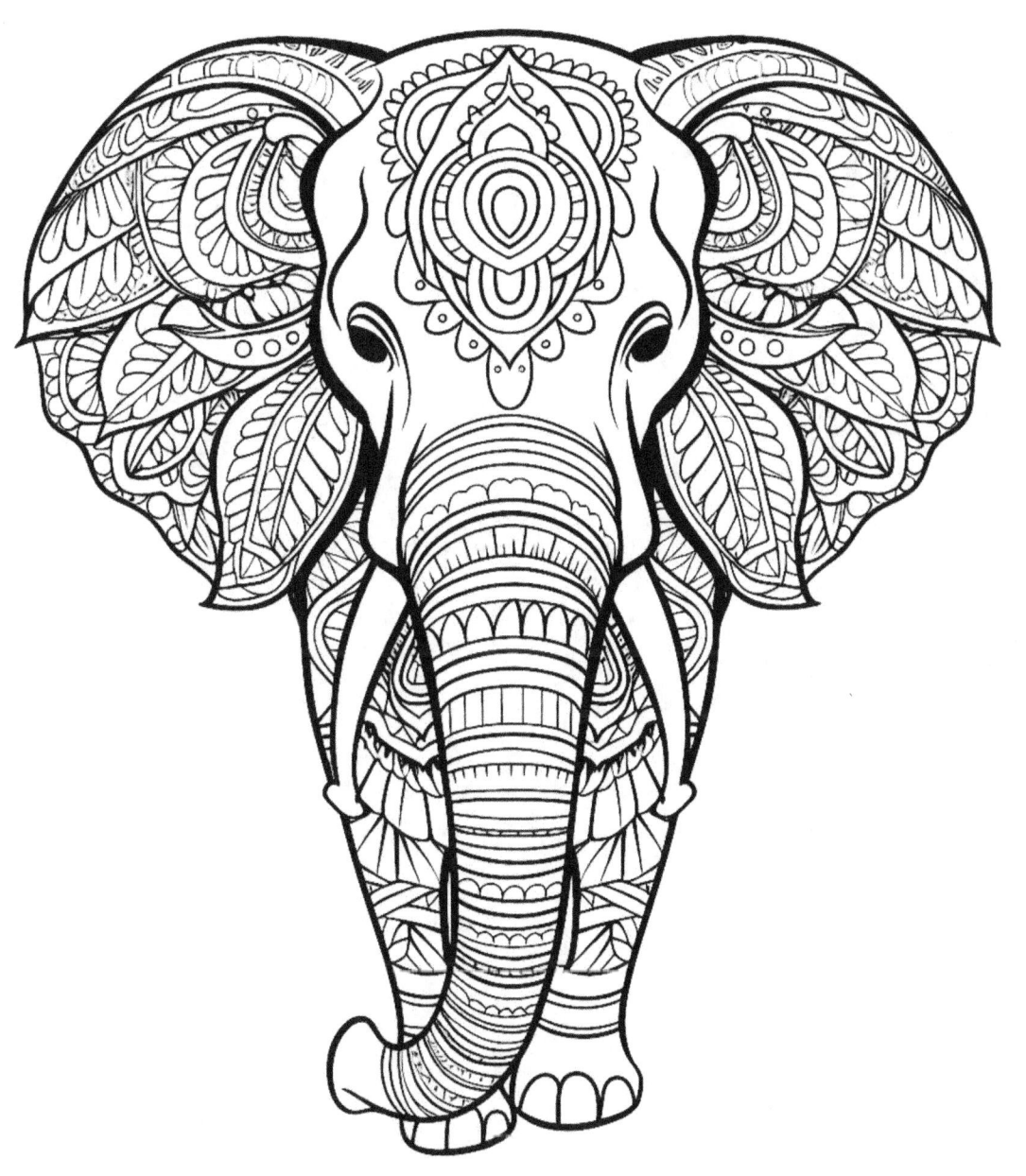

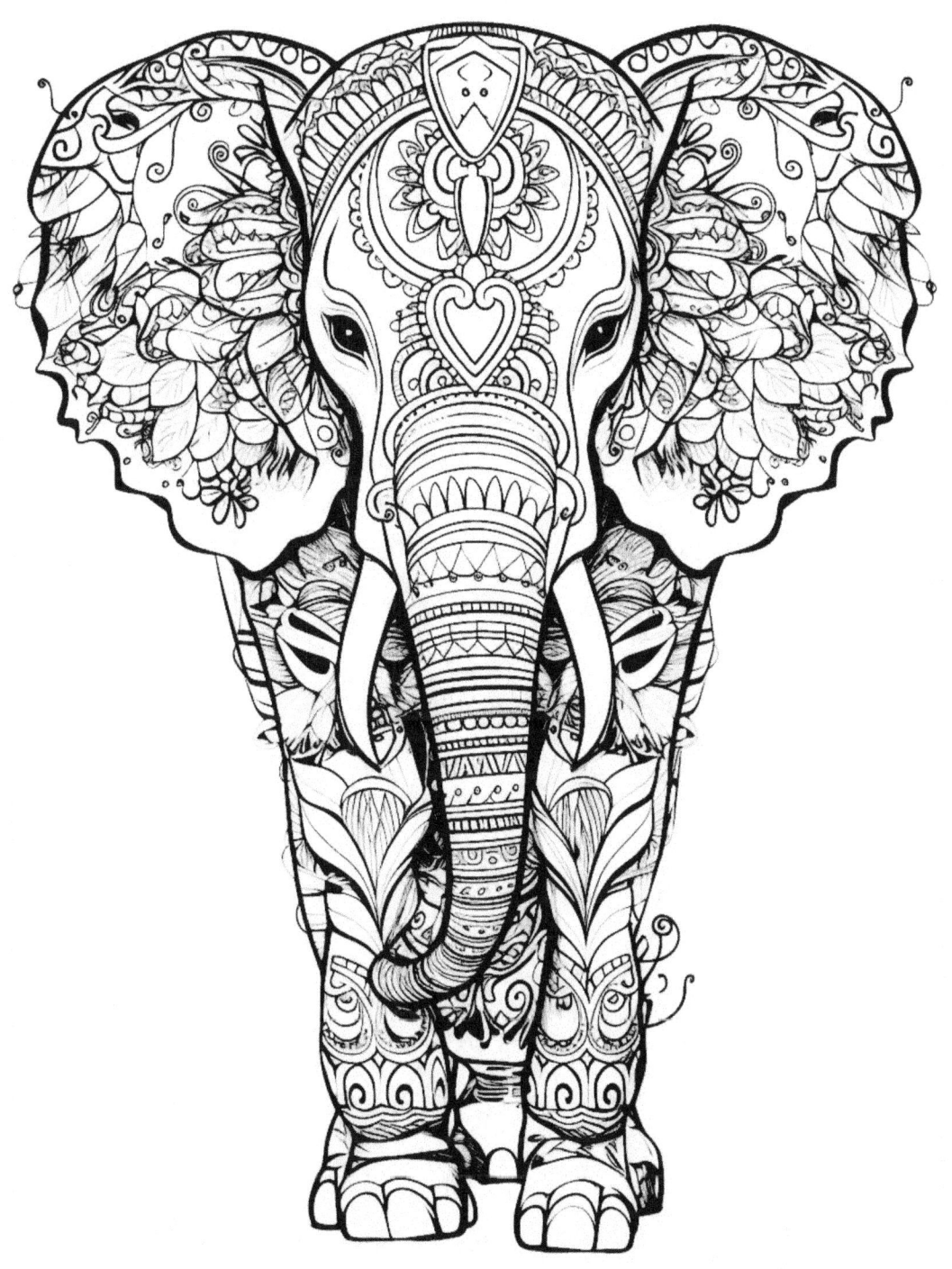

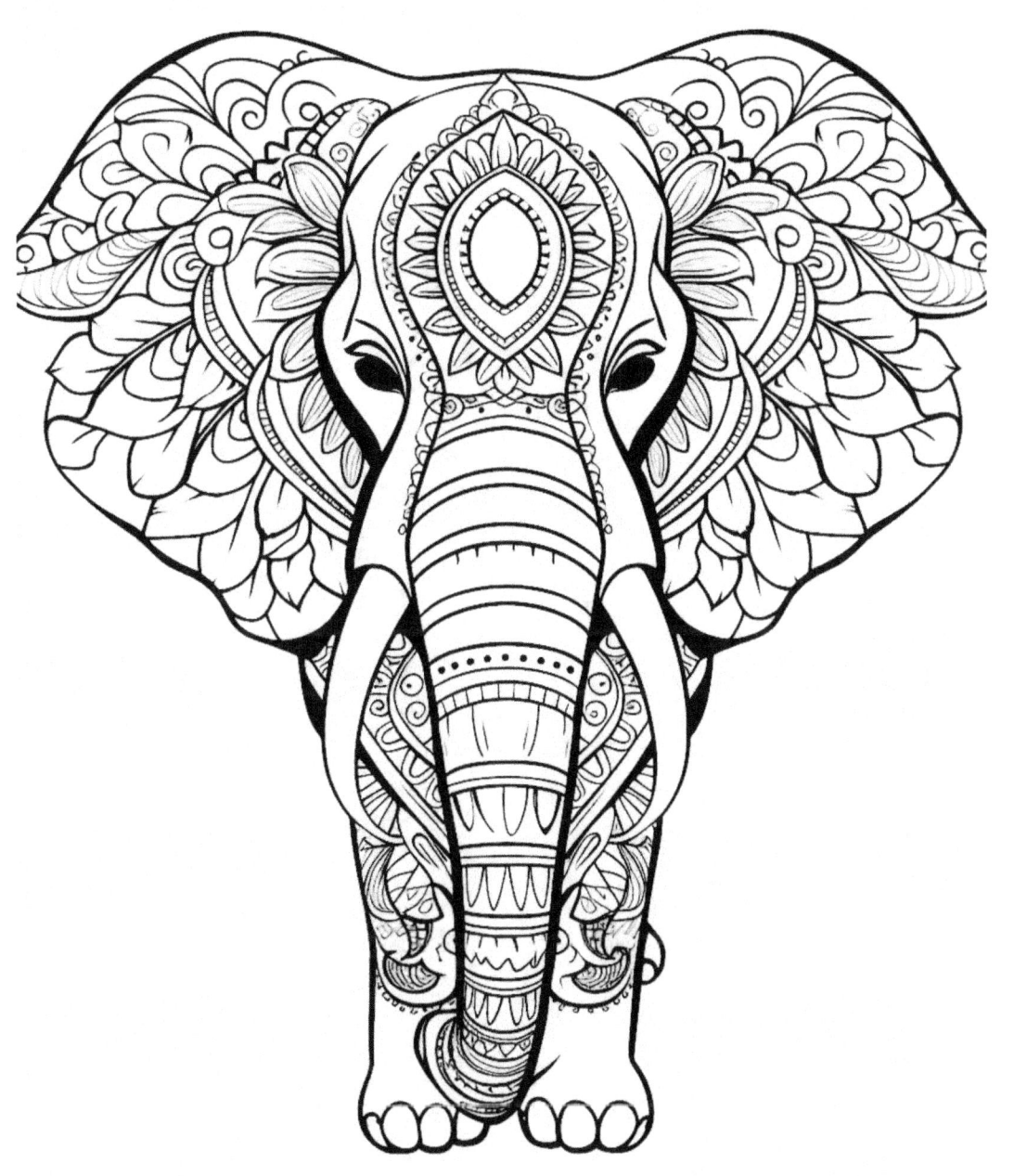

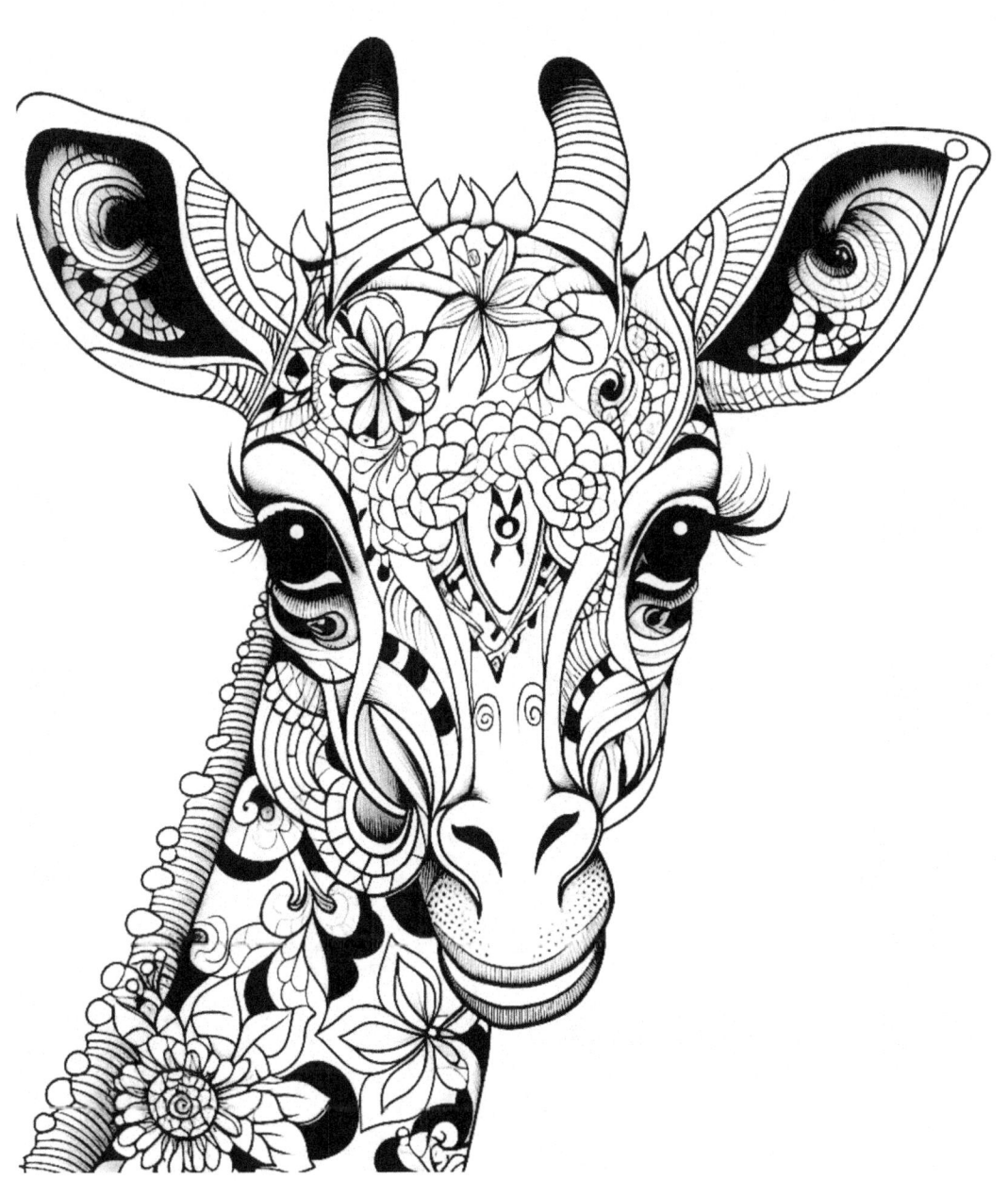

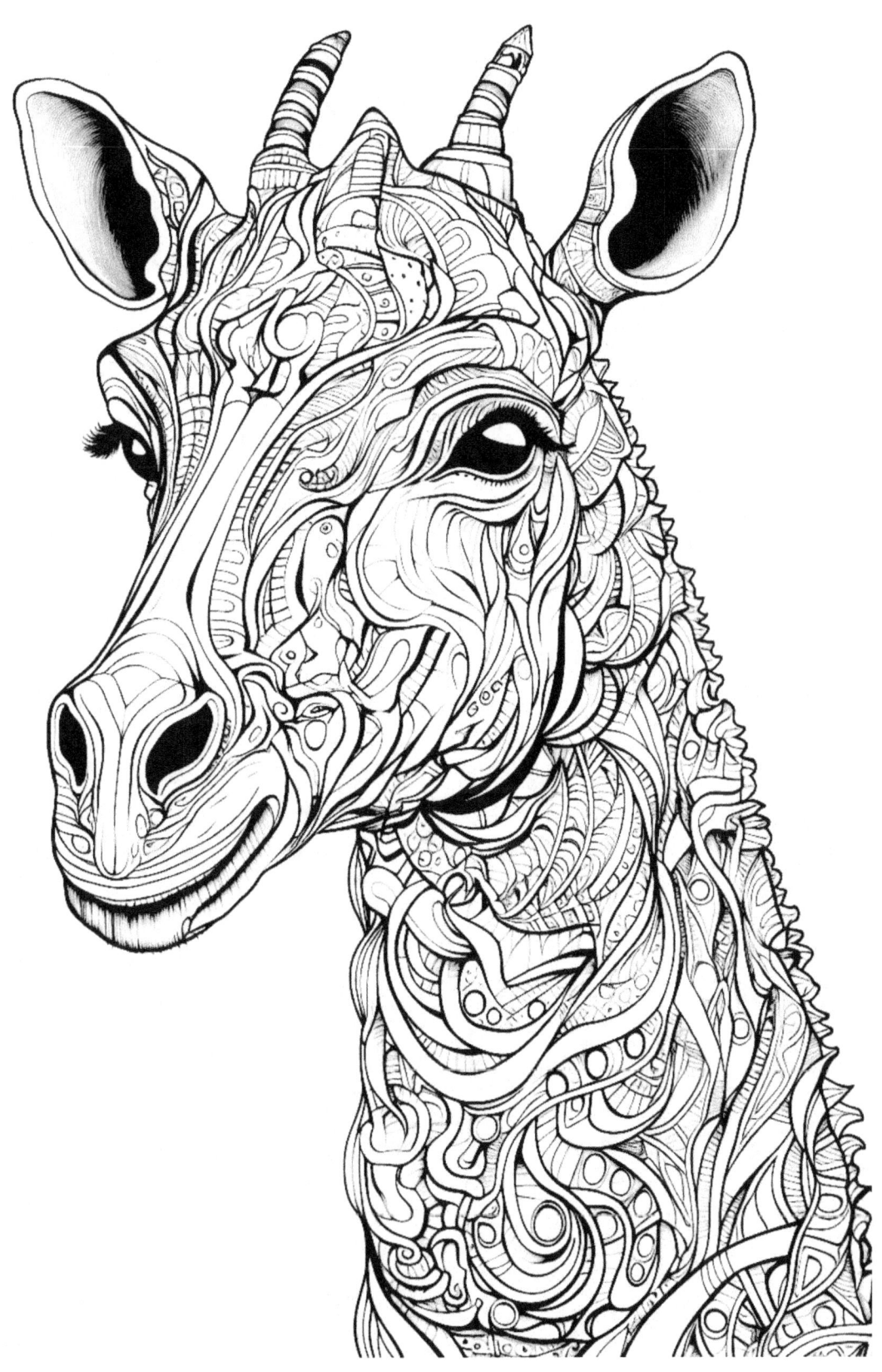

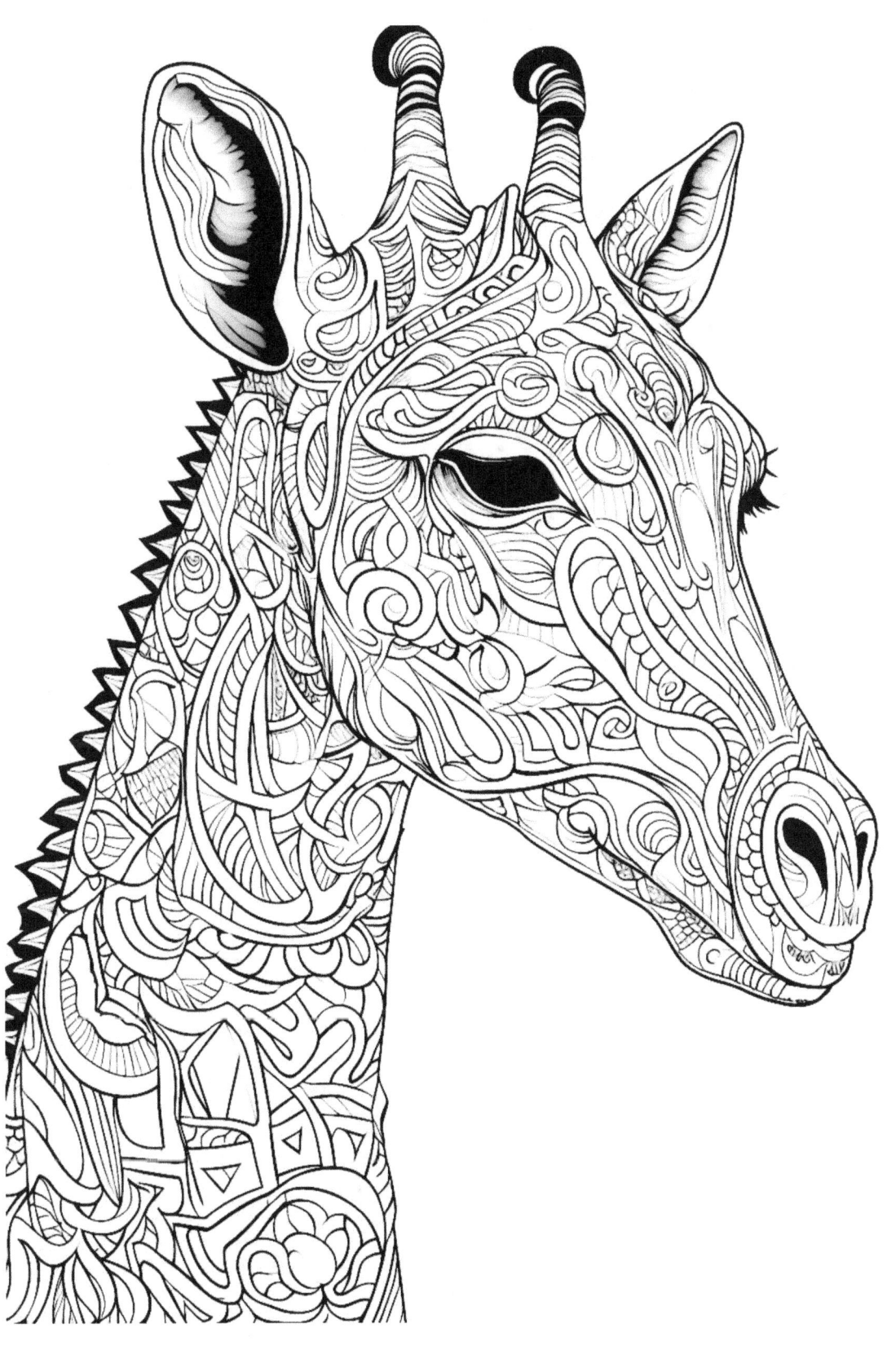

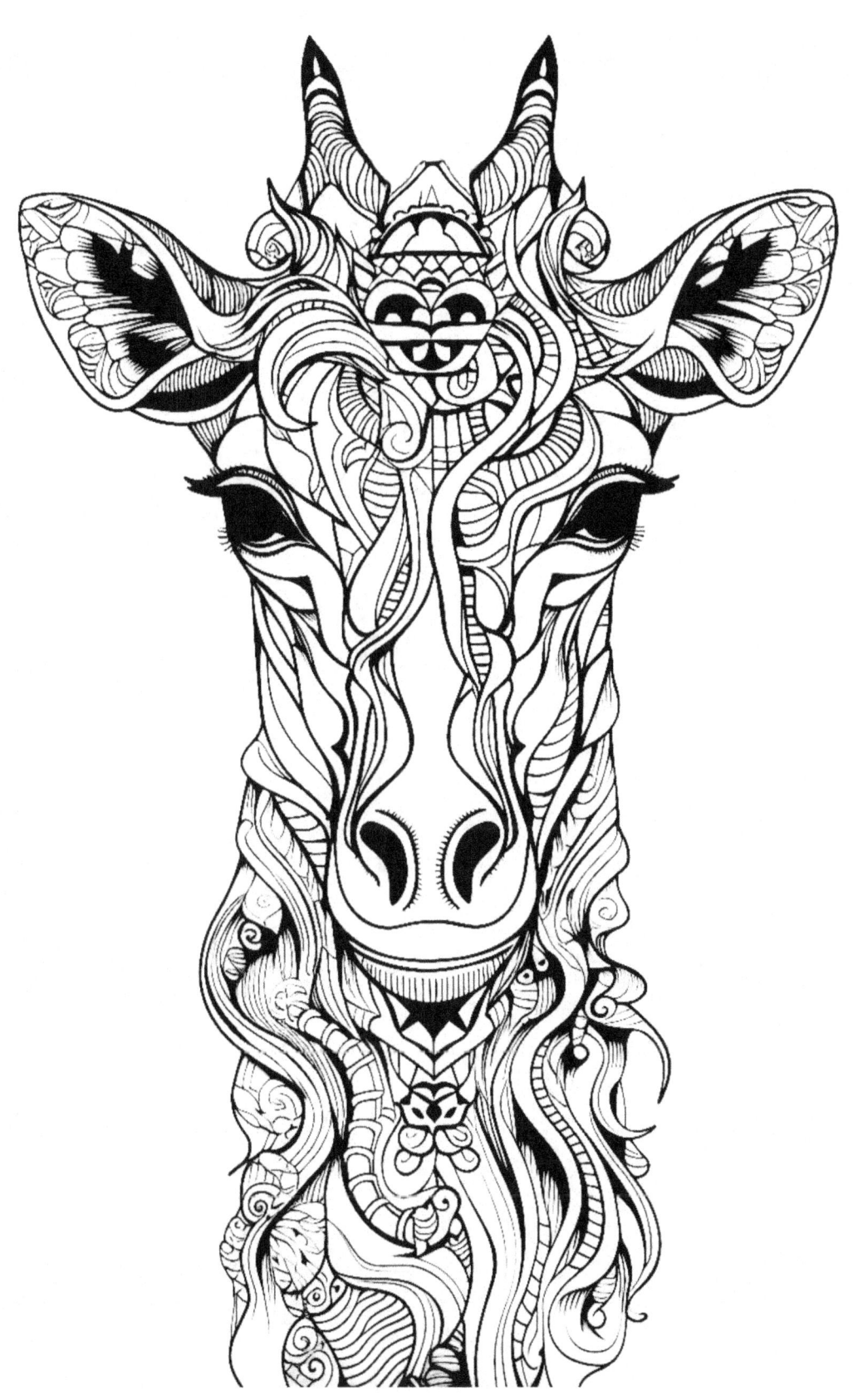

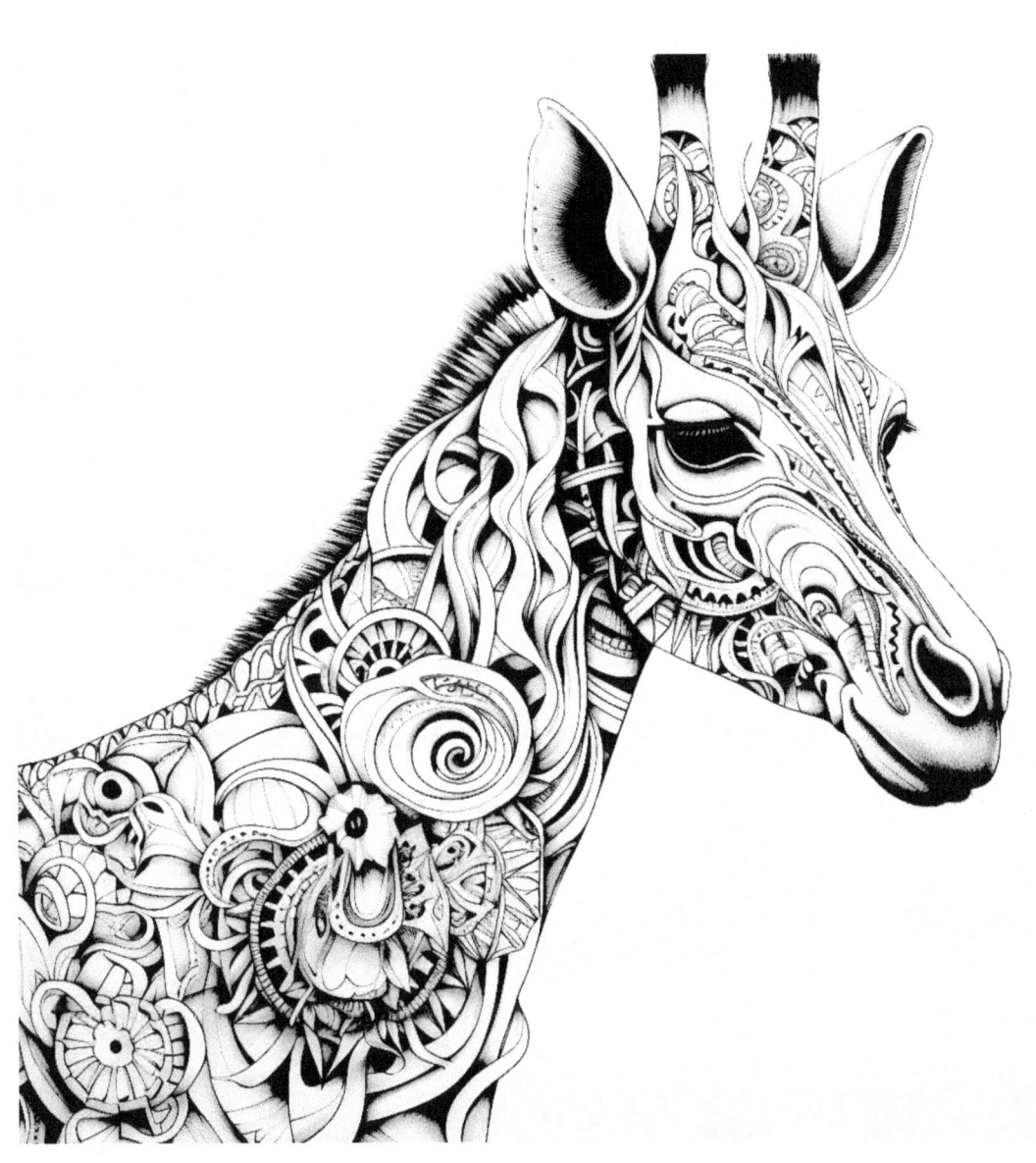

Gorilla
Rhinoceros
Beetle

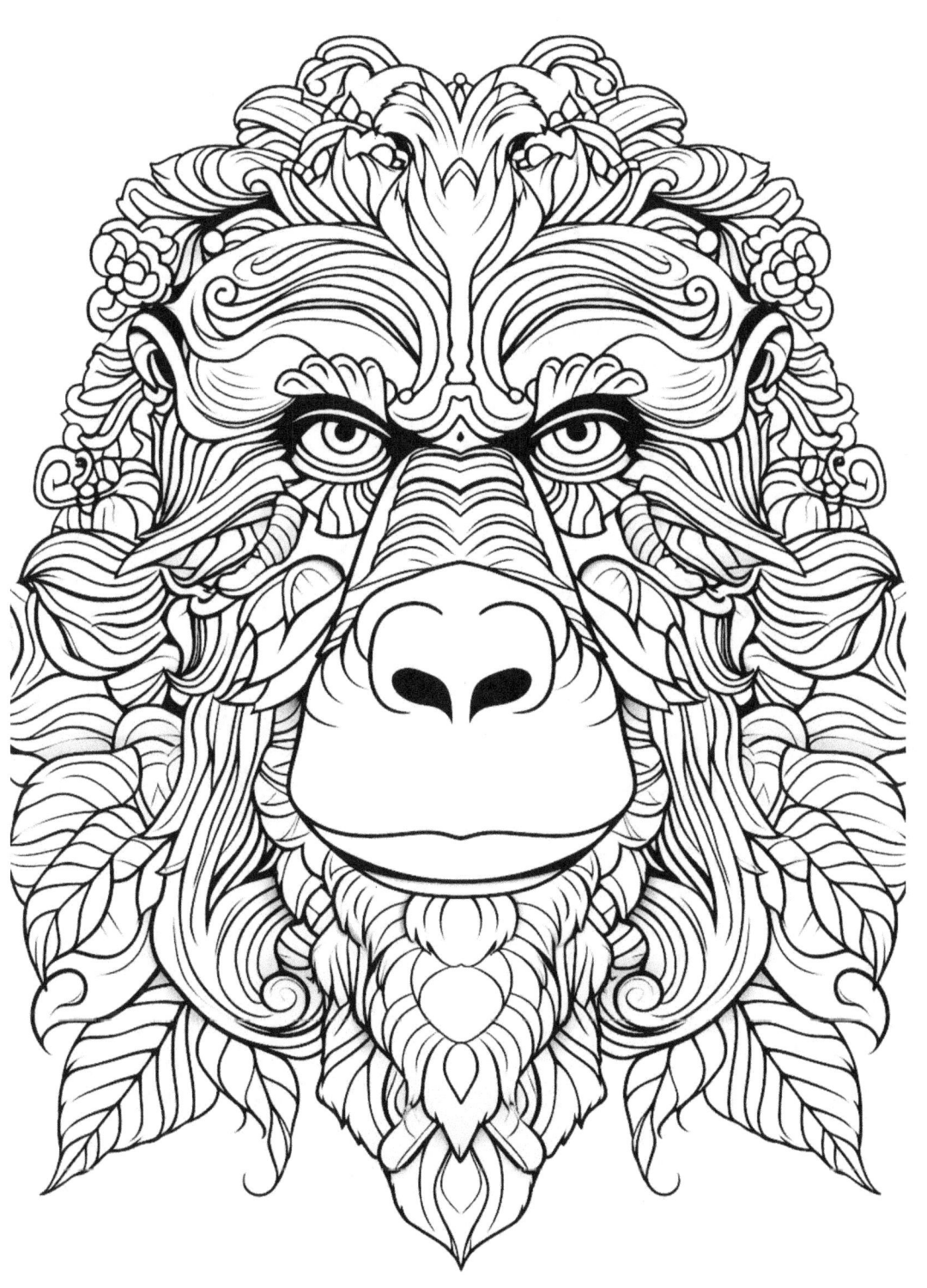

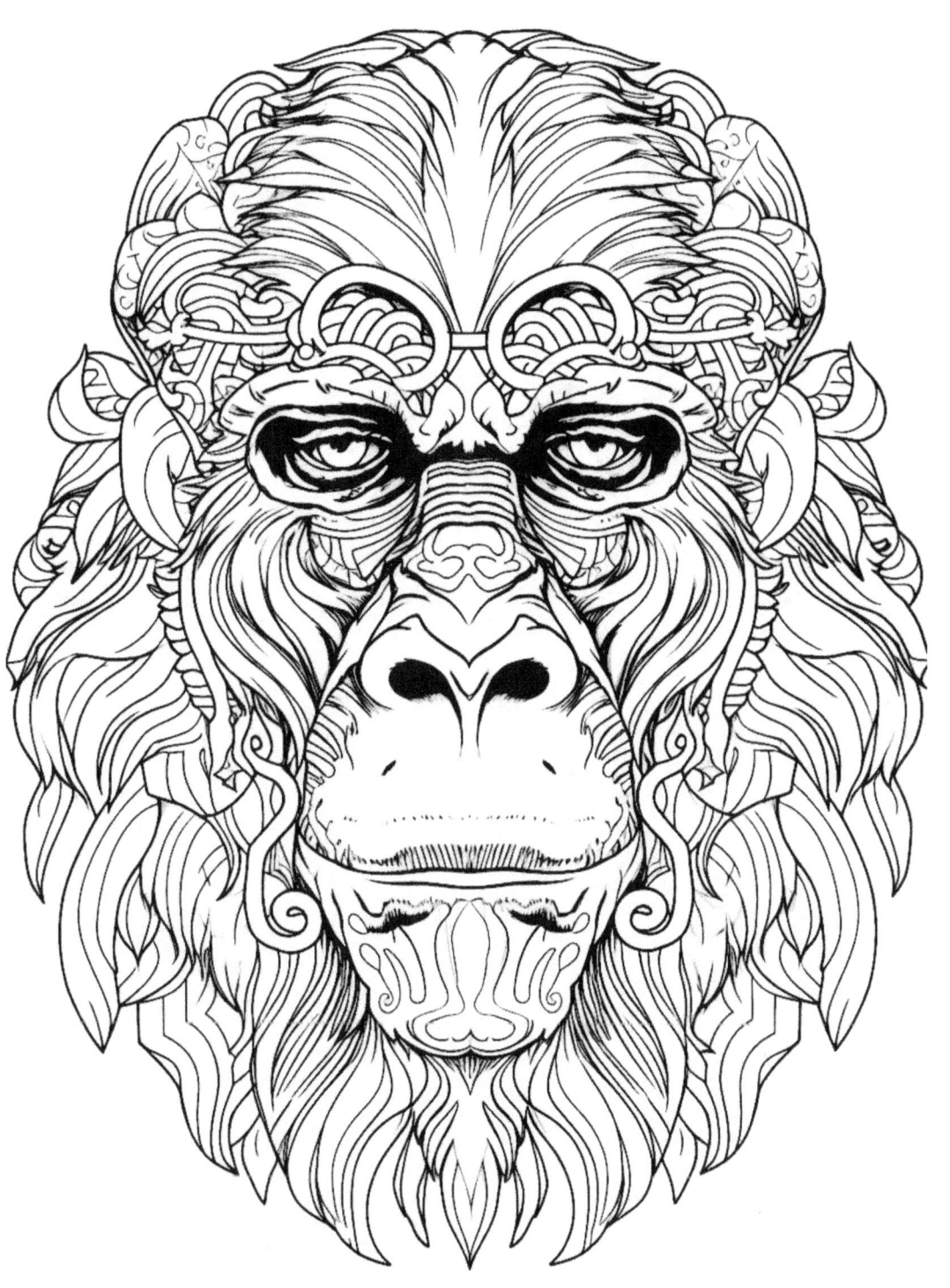

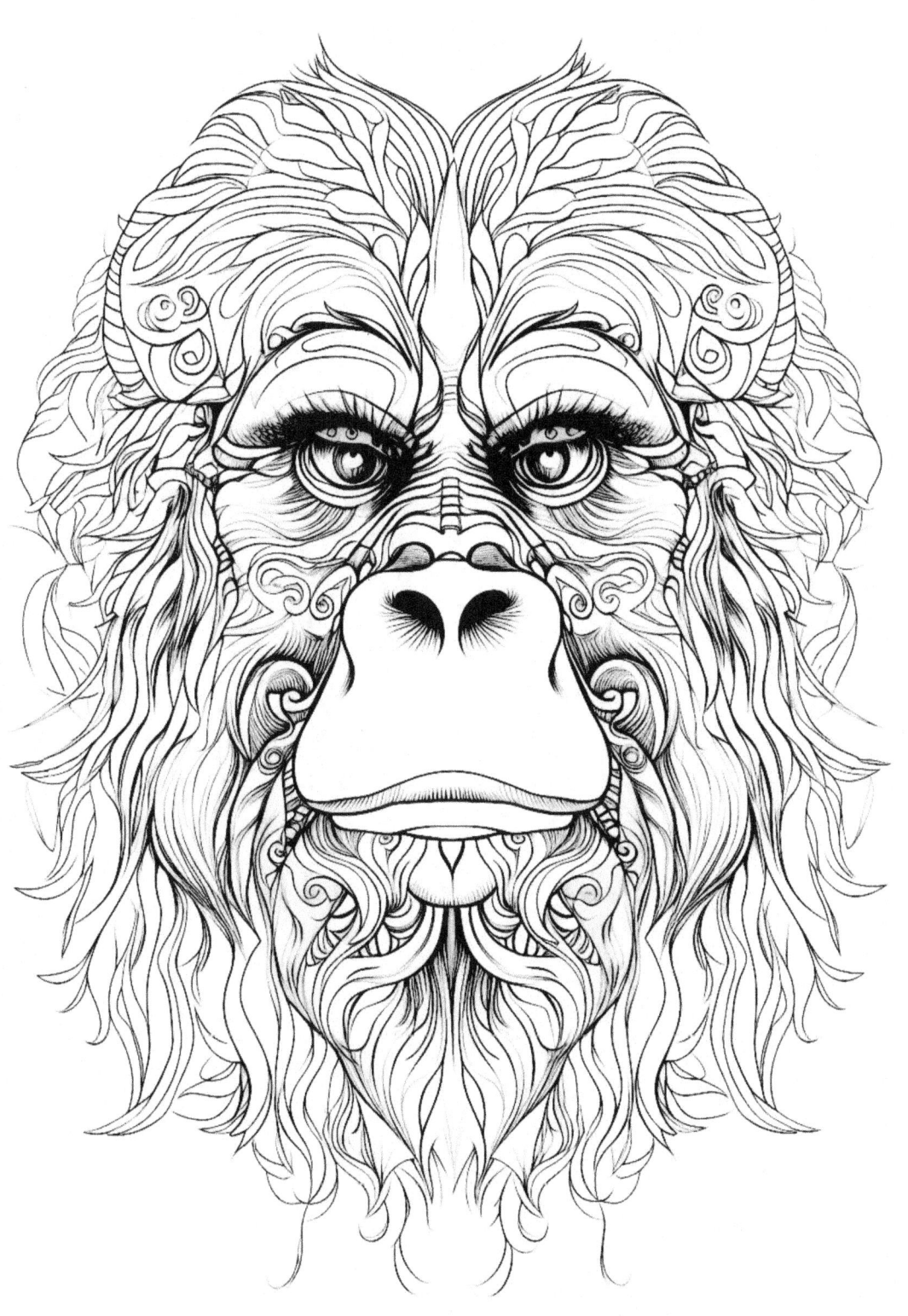

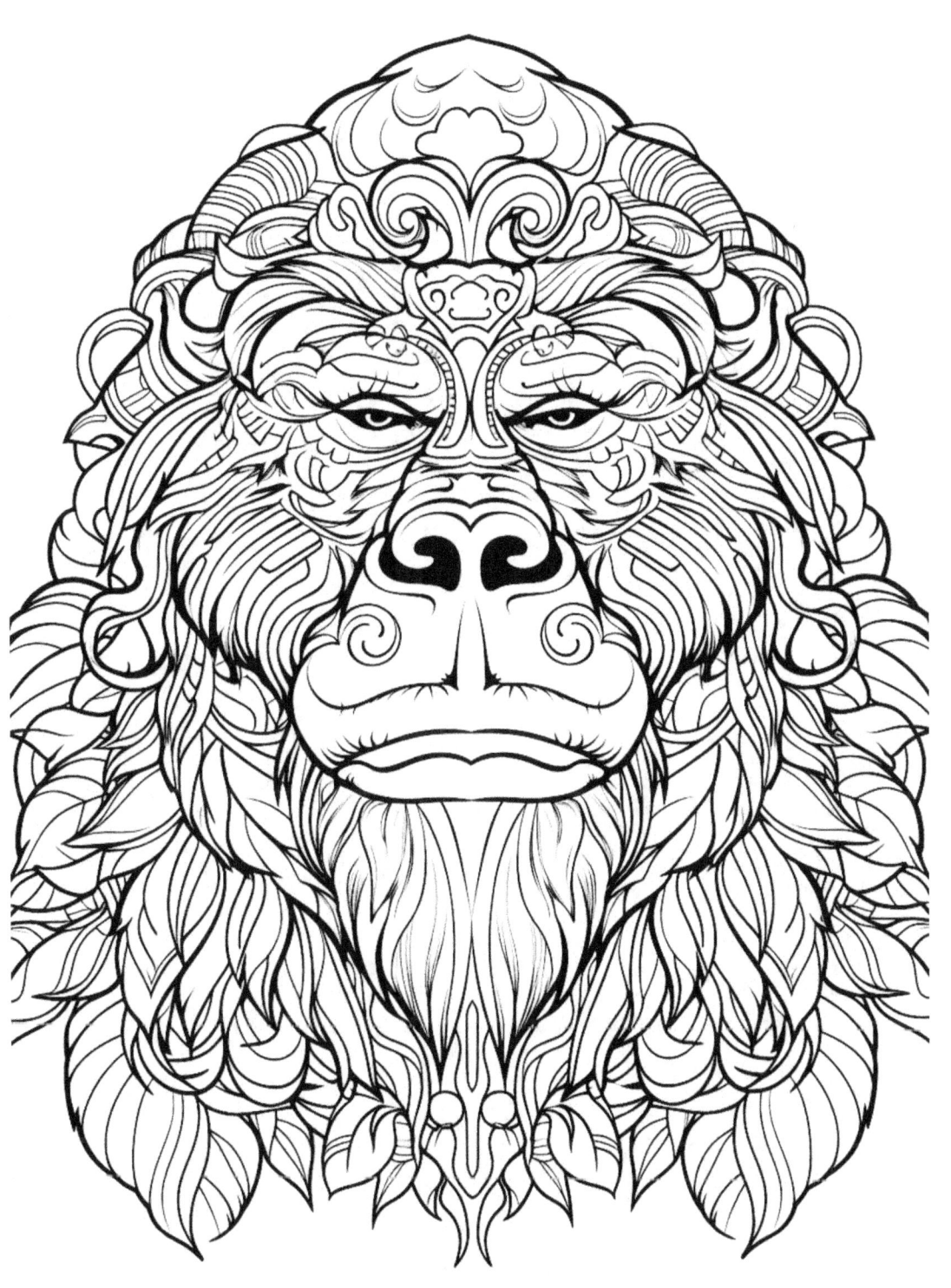

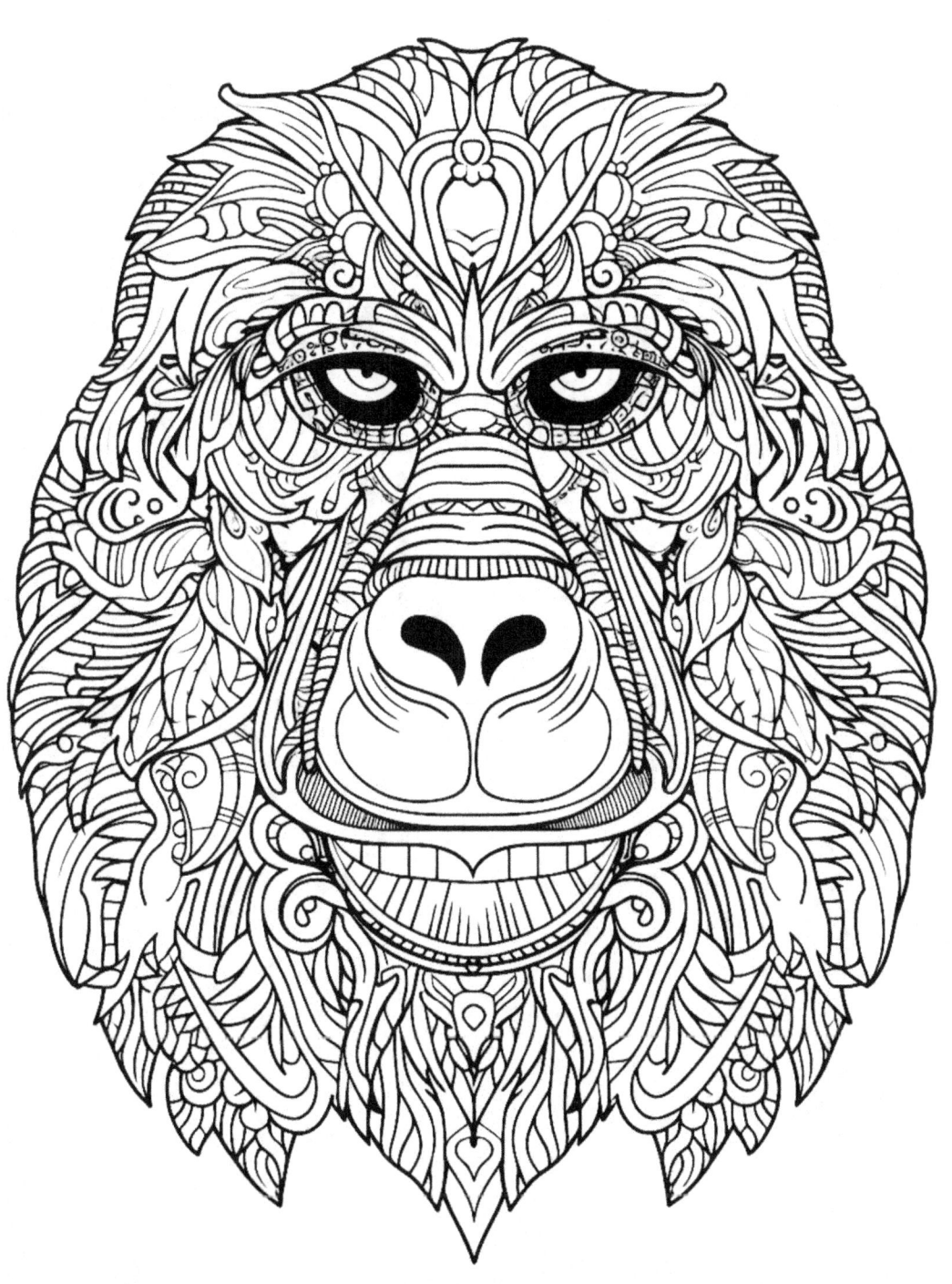

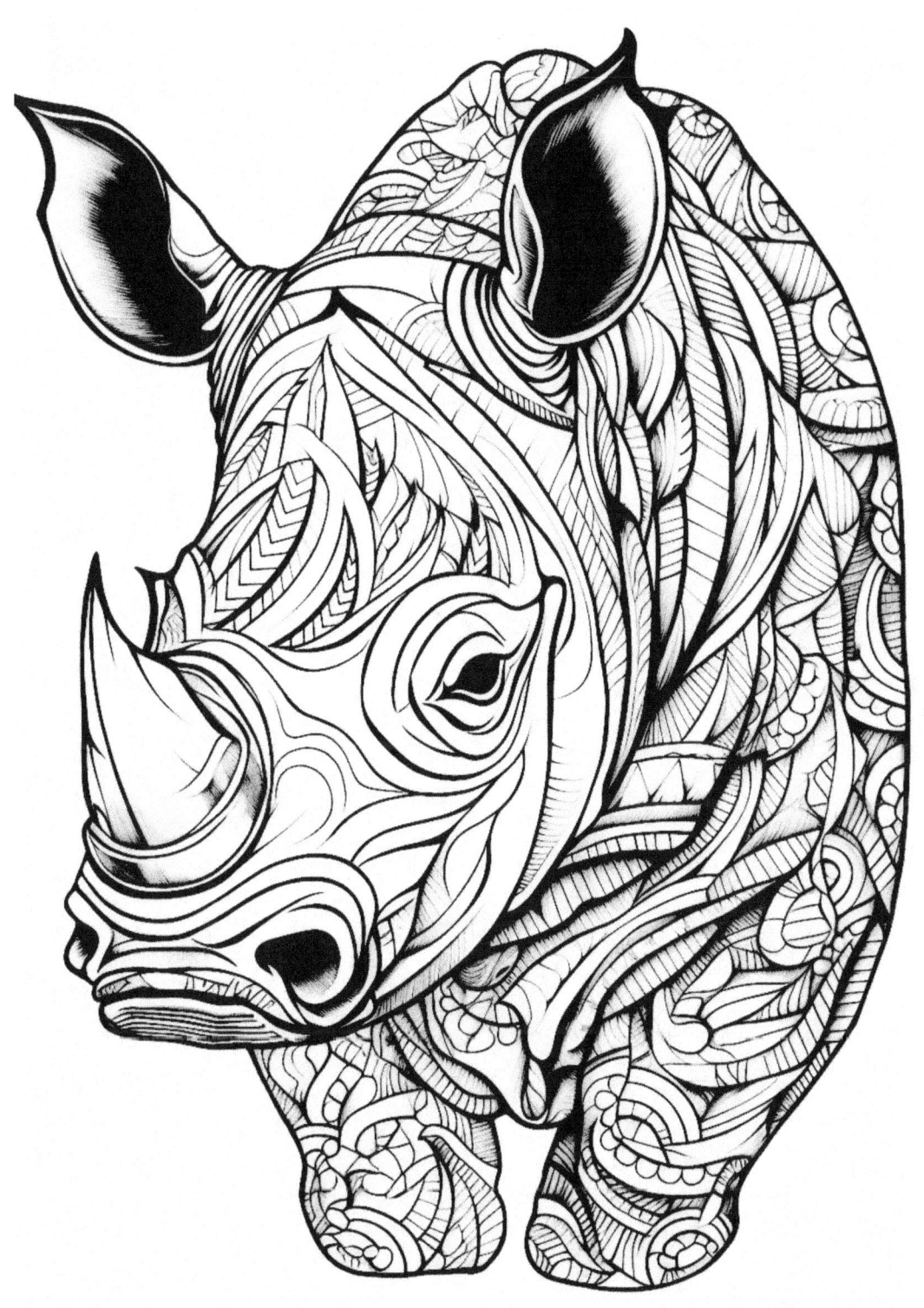

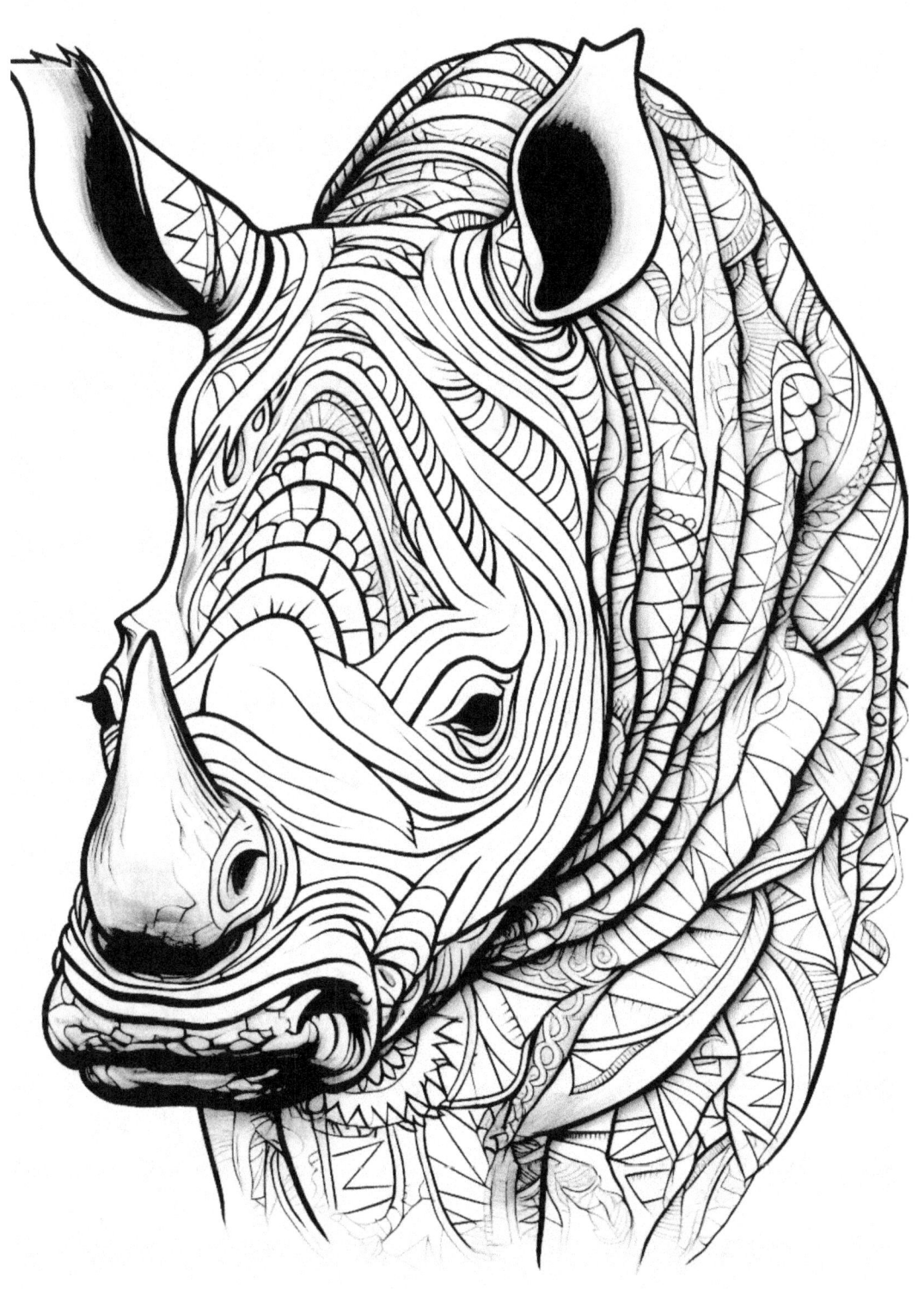

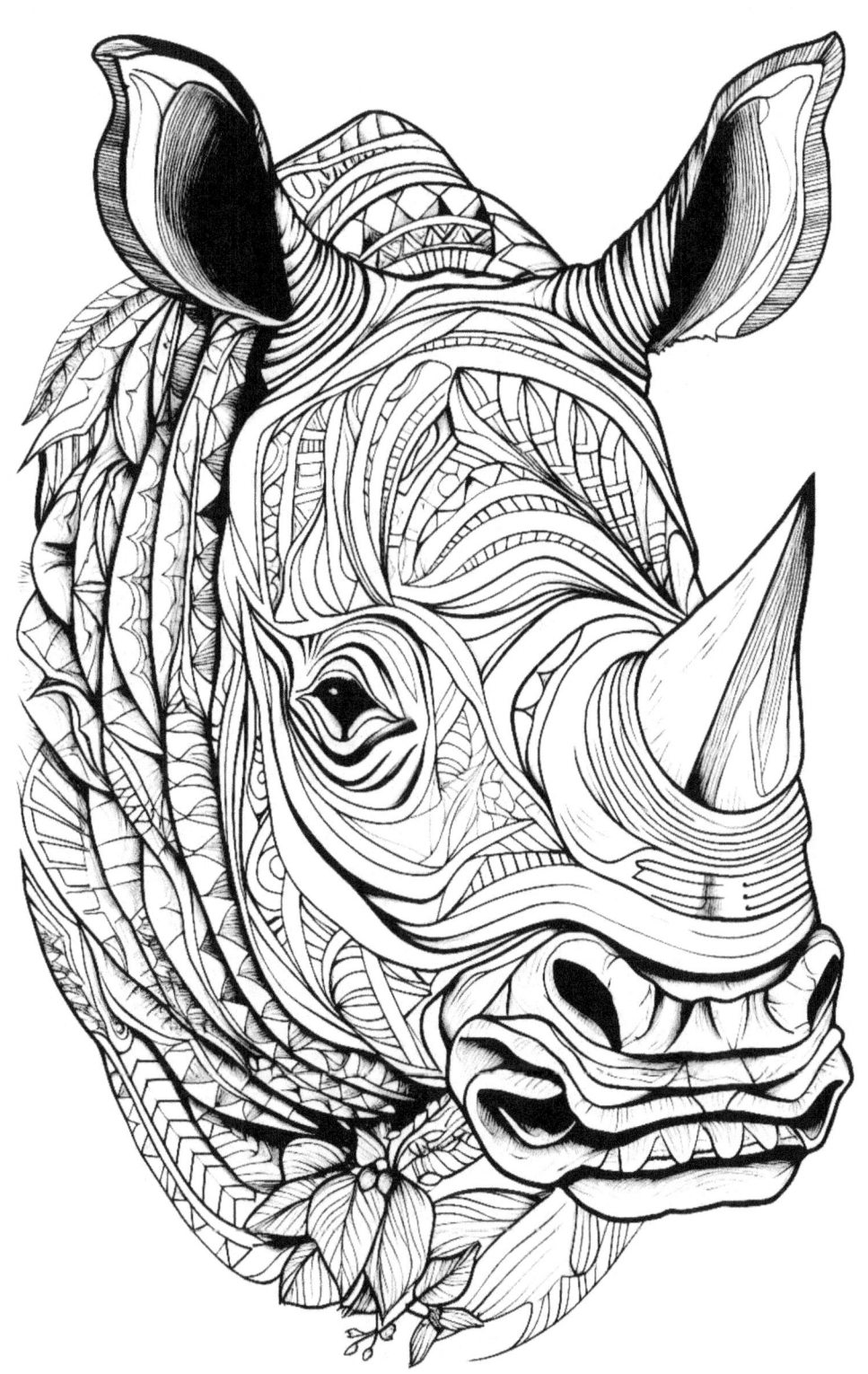

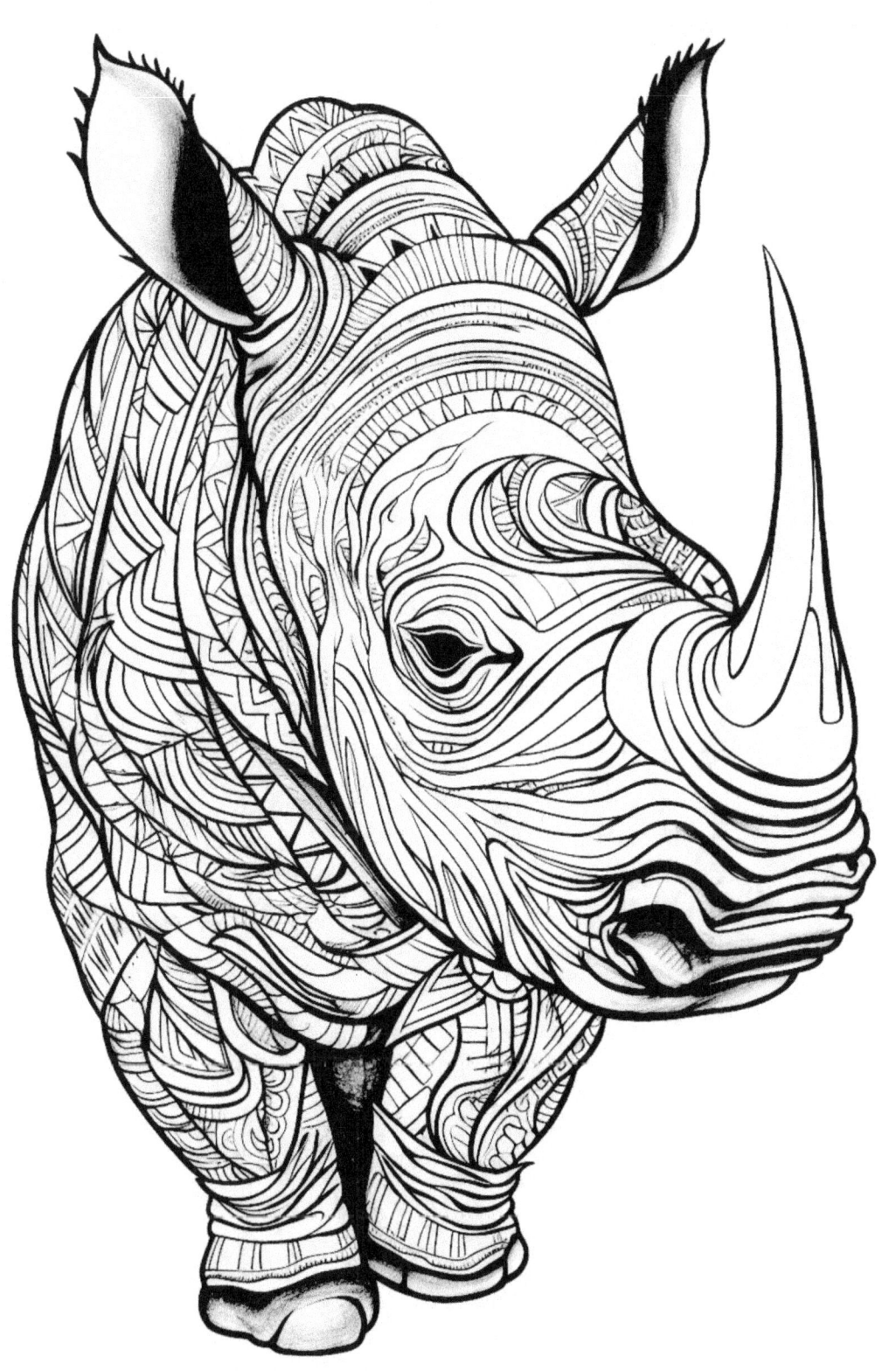

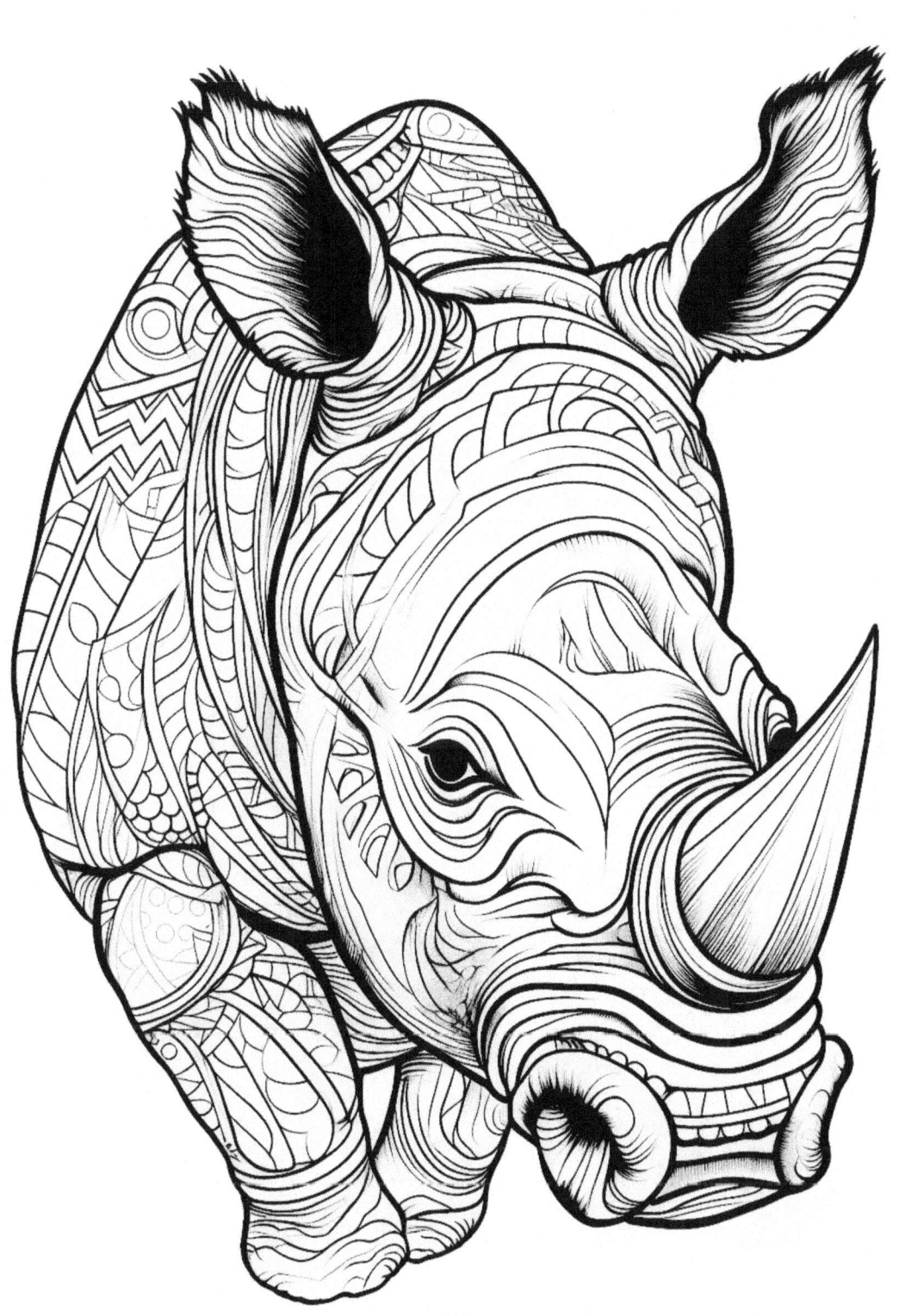

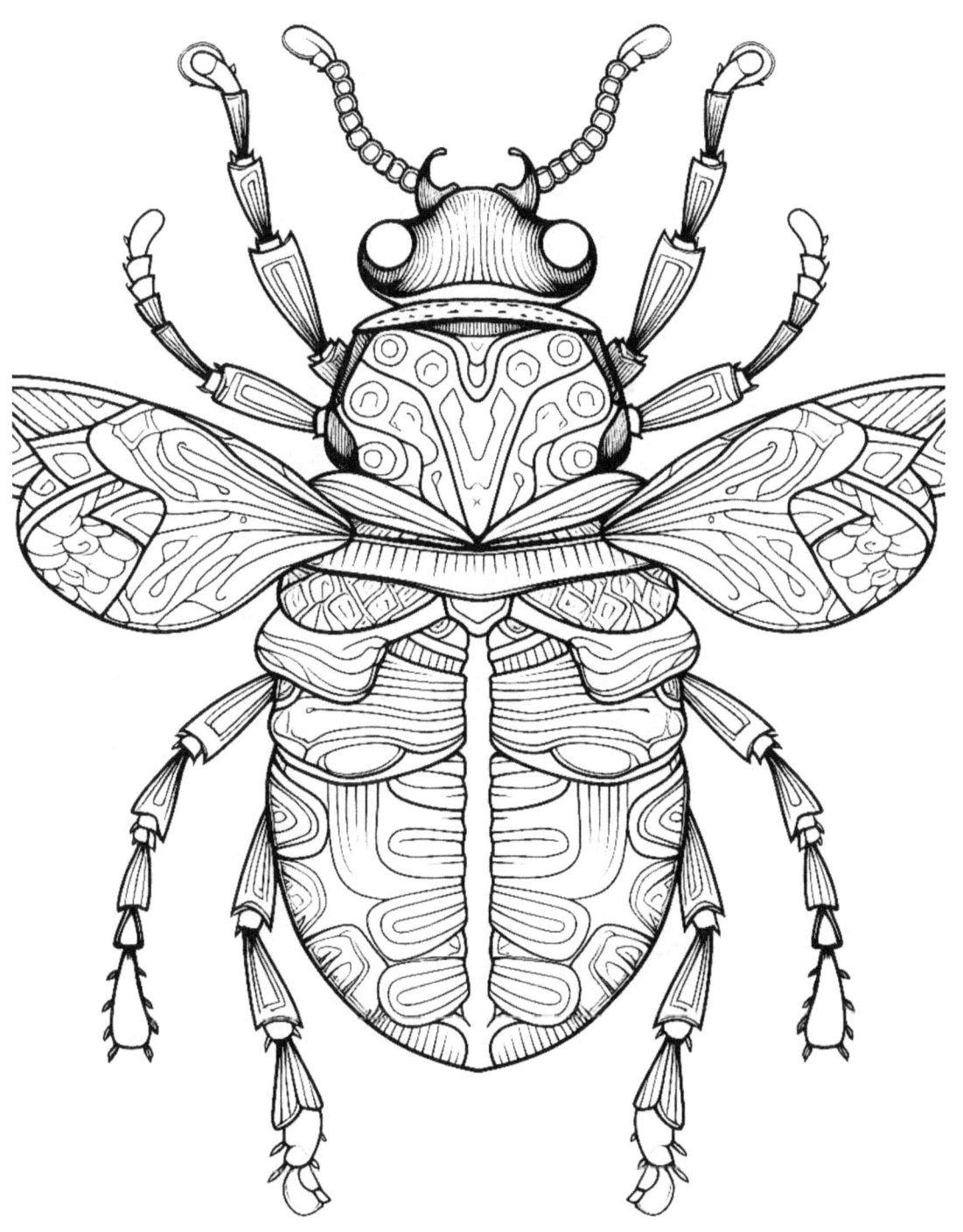

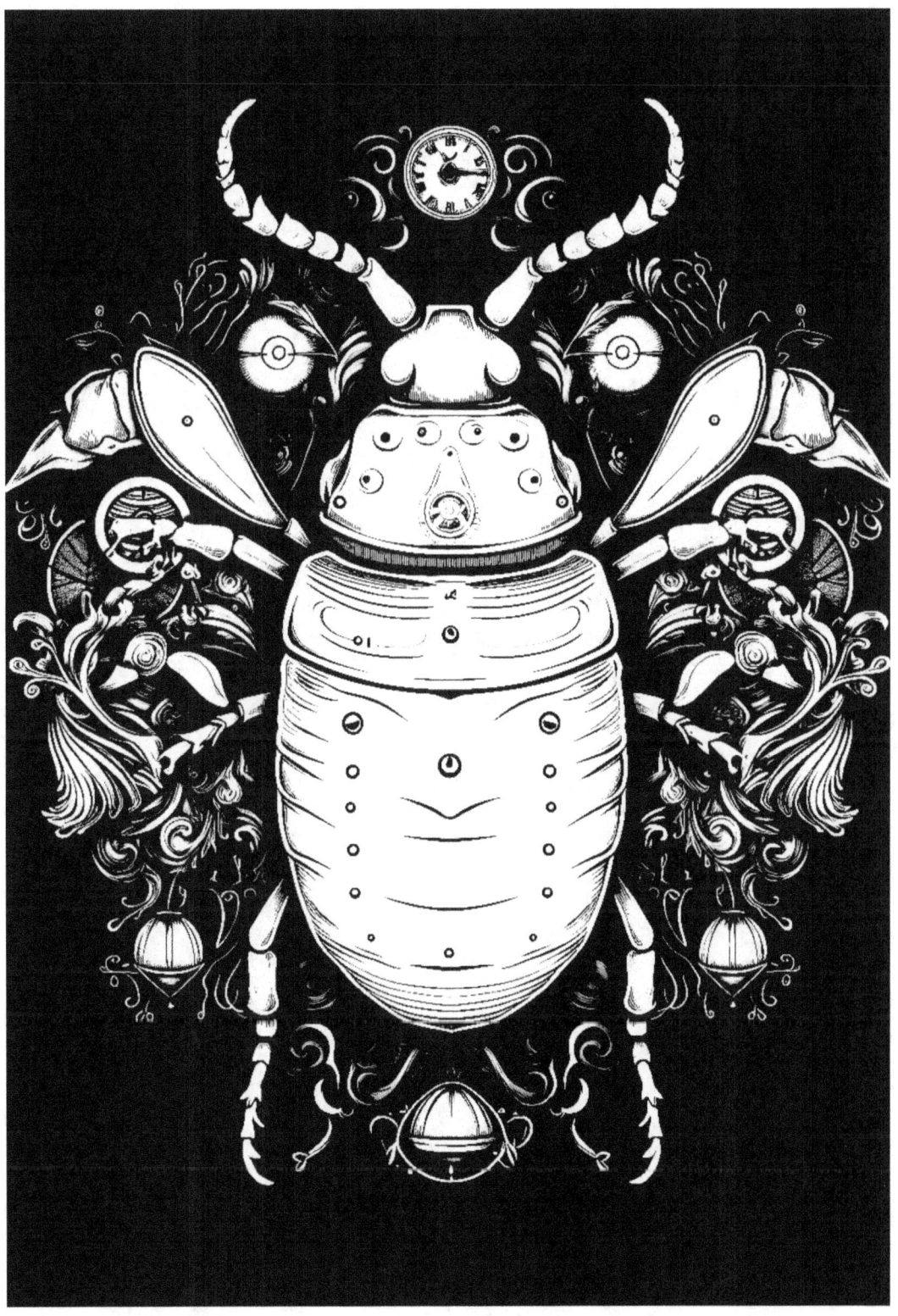

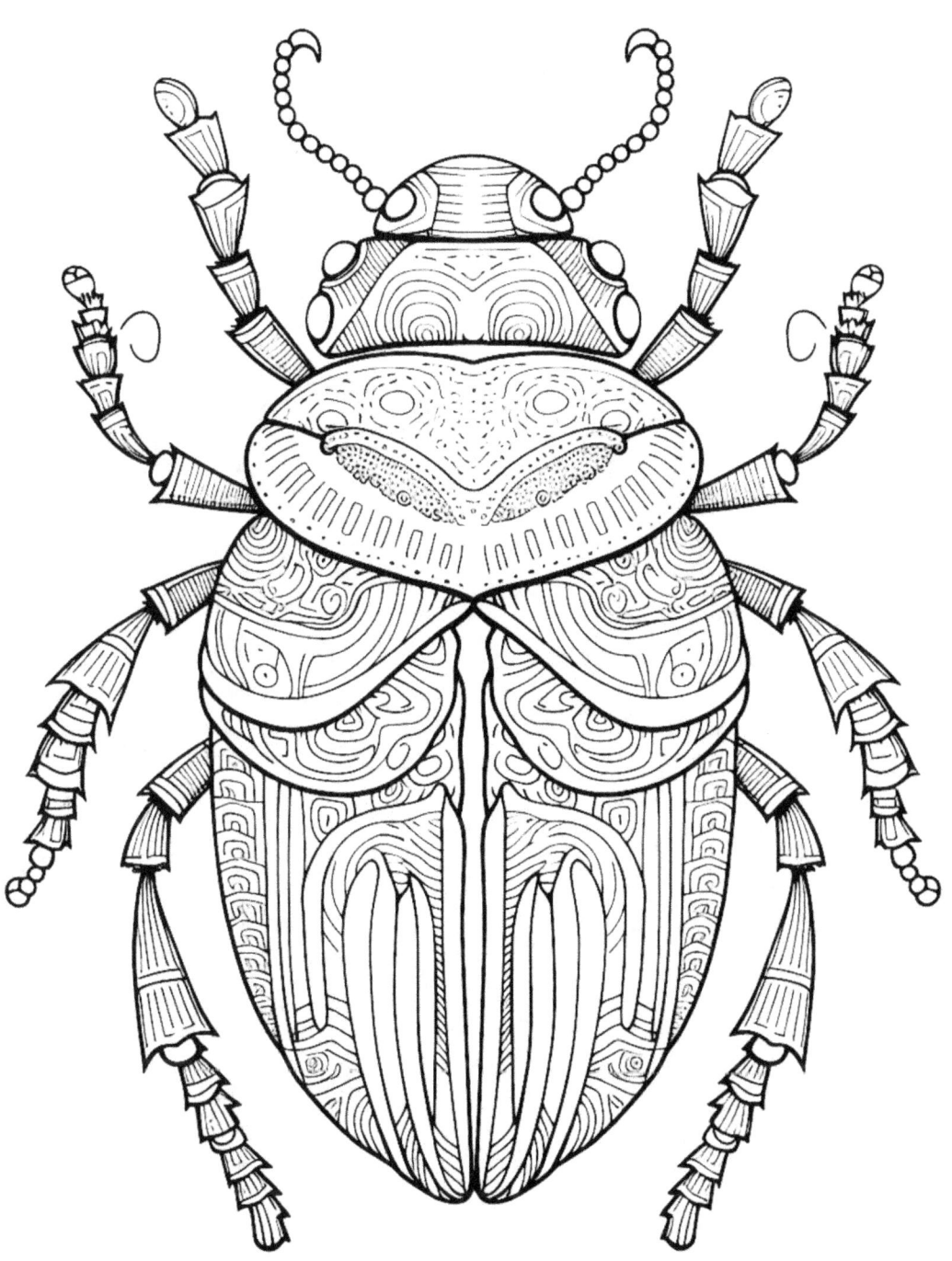

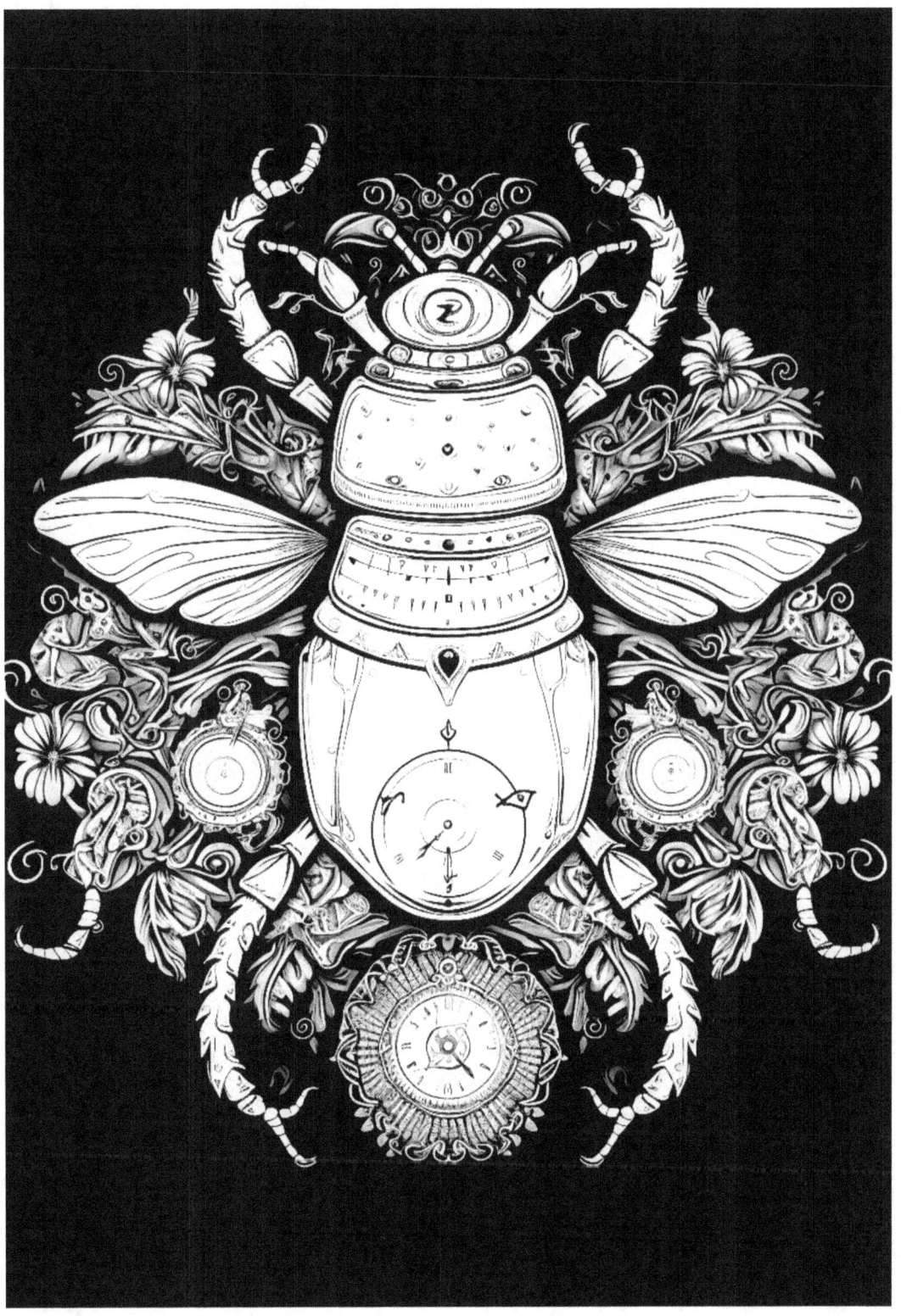

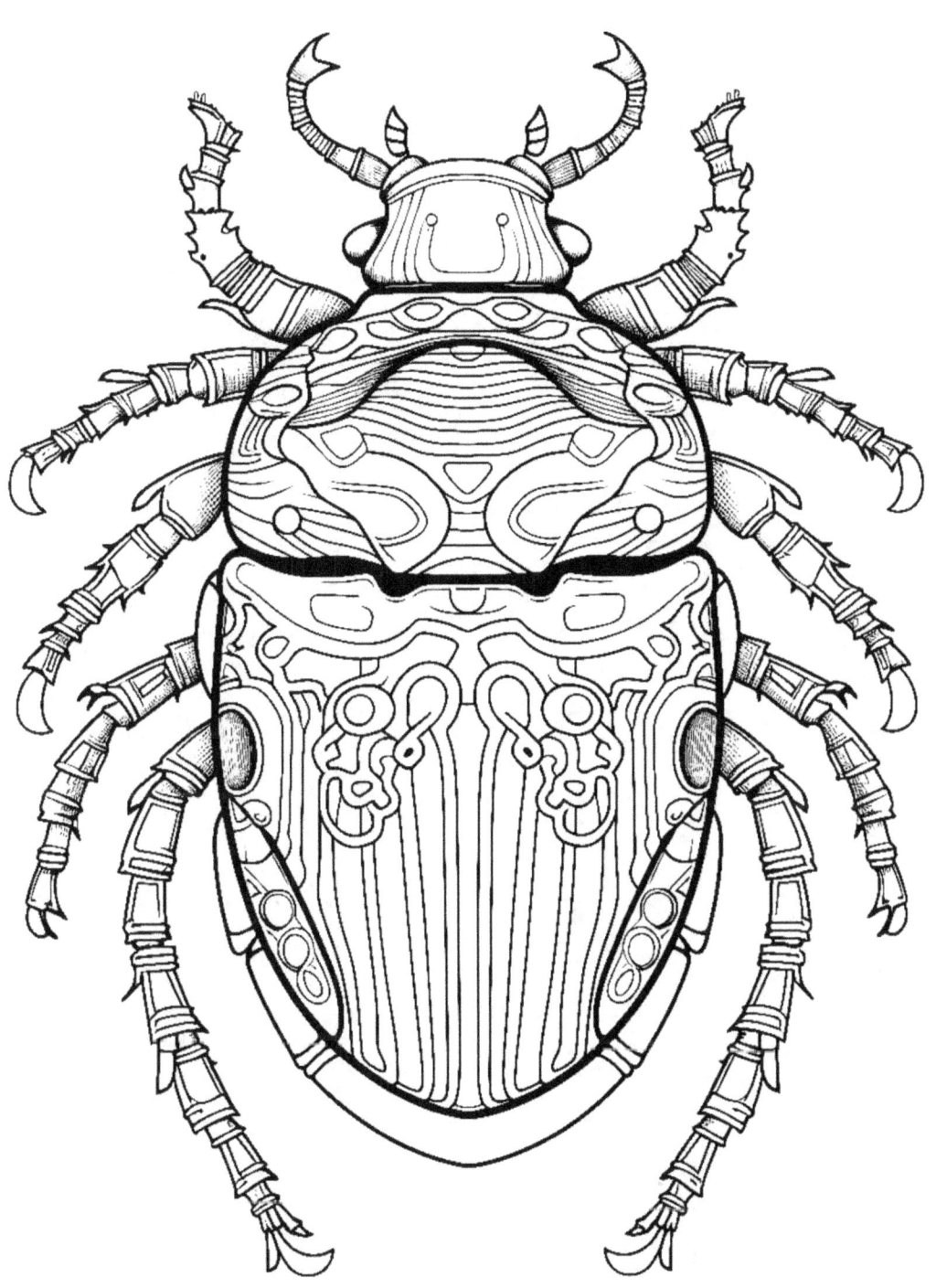